WHEN THE RIVER BURNED

WHEN THE RIVER BURNED

THE UNTOLD STORY OF THE JUPITER EXPLOSION

JOEY OLIVER

Michigan State University Press | *East Lansing*

Michigan State University Press
East Lansing, Michigan 48823-5245

Library of Congress Cataloging-in-Publication Data is available
ISBN 978-1-61186-586-8 (Paper)
ISBN 978-1-60917-837-6 (PDF)
ISBN 978-1-62895-592-7 (ePub)

Cover design by Erin Kirk
Cover photo: The *Jupiter* burns hours after exploding on the Saginaw River.

Visit Michigan State University Press at *www.msupress.org*

For Chelsea, Lorelai, Clementine, and Harrington.

As a soaking rain pelted the sailors, Hell visited the Saginaw River.

JENNI LAIDMAN, *BAY CITY TIMES*

Contents

Preface

IT STARTED WITH A SOUND—LOW, THUNDEROUS, THE KIND OF NOISE THAT MAKES people pause, uncertain of what they have just heard. A second later, the sky above Bay City, Michigan, turned black. A dense column of smoke, towering and absolute, rose above the Saginaw River, blotting out the morning light. At the smoke's source, just downstream from the Independence Bridge, the tanker ship *Jupiter* was in flames, its steel hull warped by an explosion that had ignited a portion of its 2.3-million-gallon cargo of unleaded gasoline.

The U.S. Coast Guard would later call it "unprecedented on the Great Lakes."[1] A man lost his life. Eleven others were injured. And for a moment, Bay City found itself at the center of a national crisis, as news cameras and investigators descended onto the small industrial town in search of answers. But more than three decades later, long after the ink of the numerous newspaper articles about the event faded, and well after the reels of footage from the months-long saga were packed away in storage closets, the story of the *Jupiter* disaster risks being forgotten. In fact, I only stumbled upon the story by accident.

Every obsession starts somewhere. For me, it began with childhood trips to northern Michigan. Growing up in mid-Michigan, I lived the sad irony of existing in a state known for its proximity to the Great Lakes yet being in the one spot where each of the lakes was a long drive away. When I was just a tyke, my family would occasionally drive north in the summer. And the moment we arrived, I could feel how the air seemed sharper, cleaner, as if it carried with it a memory. On the shore of Lake Superior, I'd stand still and let the spray of the waves hit my face. That lake was less a body of water than a stage: endless, unfathomable, and haunted. I remember staring out and thinking about the *Edmund Fitzgerald*—how a freighter so massive could simply vanish. And then I'd think about the other ships, hundreds of them, swallowed and held by the same waters stretching before me. For a child, that realization was staggering: the idea that something so vast could keep its secrets so close.

As a child, I was captivated by the freighters. Some stretched more than a thousand feet in length, steel leviathans of industry, but from the shoreline they appeared as nothing more than black pinpricks on the horizon. I couldn't have known it at the time, but those distant silhouettes were quietly shaping the way I understood the world: that something immense could appear so small, and that scale was always a matter of perspective.

That childhood curiosity soon became deliberate. I visited Whitefish Point, the Soo Locks, and the Valley Camp Museum, the places where the Great Lakes gave up their secrets in bits and pieces. I remember standing at the wheel of the *Valley Camp*, a retired Great Lakes freighter given new meaning, in the form of a time capsule of sorts for the industry, as a museum ship, and indulging in a kind of child's thought experiment: imagining myself on the open waters of Superior on a clear, calm day. And then flipping the thought—imagining that same helm in the middle of a storm, when the water wasn't a mirror but a threat. The difference was terrifying.

By then I was devouring everything I could find about shipwrecks: the *Carl D. Bradley*, the *Daniel J. Morrell*, and, inevitably, the *Edmund Fitzgerald.* These weren't just accidents; they were transformations, where freighters became legends. While other children were outside chasing baseballs or testing the boundaries of parental patience, I was inside watching documentaries about freighters lost to the lake, reading books about ships that disappeared under the weight of wind and water. My parents didn't discourage it. If anything, they seemed to understand that this wasn't isolation but fascination—the kind of obsession that youth sometimes requires to make sense of the world.

And the fascination didn't fade with age. In college, at Saginaw Valley State University, I rented a place in Carrollton, Michigan, just outside the city of Saginaw. The street I lived on ended at the river. That meant I had a front-row seat as the freighters came and went, loading and unloading, their slow progress downriver more mesmerizing than anything happening on campus. Soon I discovered other vantage points along M-13, scattered places where you could stand for hours, watching the giants move by. It was no longer just a childhood interest. It had become a way of seeing—a lens through which the everyday acquired its own scale and weight.

One afternoon, almost by accident, I came across Ric Mixter, a journalist and historian from mid-Michigan whose reputation in maritime circles is almost mythic. Mixter had gone down to the lake bottoms themselves, diving on the wreck of the *Edmund Fitzgerald* and dozens of other vessels. He wasn't just knowledgeable about the Great Lakes—he embodied the region's memory, cataloging its disasters with the precision of an archivist and the curiosity of a storyteller. Mixter hosted a podcast, *Maritime Mixtories*, which I began to binge during the most ordinary of moments—folding laundry, doing the dishes, or cleaning up the messes left behind by young children as my house transformed from a neat place of relaxation and into a playground for my children. And it was in that context that I heard something that stopped me cold: the story of the explosion of the *Jupiter*.

I knew about shipwrecks. About captains steering into storms and crews swallowed by Superior's waves. But an oil tanker exploding in the middle of the Great Lakes' shipping routes? That was something different. The story refused to leave me alone.

When I dug deeper, the strangeness only grew. There were no books. No documentaries. Just fragments: a long series of front-page stories from the *Bay City Times*, grainy television footage of flames clawing into the sky. Mixter himself admitted that it was this very coverage—the sight of a freighter on fire—that first drew him into maritime history.[2] And there it was again: the pattern. A great disaster, briefly the focus of obsessive attention, allowed to slip into the background half-forgotten, as though the fire had consumed not only the ship but its place in collective memory. As the years passed, the story faded. It became another piece of forgotten history, revisited only on anniversaries—if at all. That's why I set out to write this story. To bring the *Jupiter* back to life.

On the surface, the story of the *Jupiter* is simple enough: a gasoline tanker exploded while unloading fuel in September of 1990. A tragic accident, quickly explained by a headline. But look a little closer, and the story changes. The *Jupiter* wasn't just about one ship, one pier, one unlucky moment. It was about what happens when systems designed to work in harmony—machines, procedures, people—fall out of alignment in just the wrong way.

And that's where the details matter. Every disaster has a prologue, a string of small, almost imperceptible decisions and oversights that, taken together, bend the narrative toward catastrophe. The *Jupiter* is no exception. To understand it, you can't just study the ship. You need to look at passing vessels, at the pier where the ship was moored, at the Saginaw River itself, and at the community of people who depended on all three. This isn't just the story of an explosion. It's the story of a system—complicated, interconnected, fragile—coming undone.

Think of it this way: The Saginaw River is not just a river. Chapter 1 of this book details how the river is really a fifteen-thousand-year-old pathway that became an artery of Michigan industry: first, the necessities of life, then the lumber boom. Later, it was reshaped by industry and then scarred by pollution. That industry is what brought the *Jupiter* to the Saginaw River on that fateful Sunday.

The gasoline in the *Jupiter*'s tanks was itself part of a much larger story—the petrochemical empire that began in the nineteenth century with John D. Rockefeller's refineries in Cleveland, and that continues to fuel both economic growth and environmental damage across the Great Lakes region. As chapter 2 shows, the environmental risks were not the only hazards; the ships themselves and their crews were also put in precarious situations at times, just by what their cargo included.

And there is yet another thread, one that stretches into the present: the long, unsettling history of contamination—"forever chemicals" that linger in soil and water, altering ecosystems and human health alike. Chapters 3 and 4 break down how local fire departments responded to the blazing ship but did not have the equipment nor the training to deal with such an incident. This meant they had to call in outside help and a company whose primary tool included firefighting foam that was made up of, in part, per- and polyfluoroalkyl substances (PFAS). These chapters also detail how this has been a theme, both on the Great Lakes and beyond. The *Jupiter* was about fire. PFAS are about persistence. But they are connected by the same theme: what happens when industrial progress leaves a legacy it can't easily erase.

The final chapters explain the National Transportation Safety Board's (NTSB's) investigation into the incident. What happened? Who was responsible? What recommendations needed to be made to ensure it didn't happen again? Lastly, were those recommendations implemented? As this book shows, many were not.

The *Jupiter* is not just an accident report. It's a parable. A window into how the Great Lakes have been used, reshaped, and tested over centuries. A single ship, one explosion, and suddenly you can see the whole system—its heroics, its tragedies, its resilience, and its flaws. In that sense, the *Jupiter* is less a story about a forgotten disaster than a reminder. It tells us that to understand the Great Lakes, you don't just look at the water. You look at what happened when it caught fire.

Chapter 1

Not Just a River

MORE THAN JUST A BODY OF WATER, THE SAGINAW RIVER IS A STORYTELLER, A SILENT witness to the unfolding drama of industry, ambition, and change. Stretching more than twenty-two miles, it begins where the Tittabawassee and Shiawassee Rivers converge. From there, it winds its way north, carrying with it the markings from the logging era and the remnants of a growing industrial presence before finally surrendering to the vast expanse of Saginaw Bay and, beyond that, Lake Huron.

To understand the presence of the Saginaw River, one must understand why Michigan looks the way it does. The answer lies not in the river itself, but in a million-year-old drama that played out on a continental stage. During the Pleistocene Epoch, glaciers came and went across North America. The most recent of these, the Wisconsin glaciation, left the deepest mark. Imagine a sheet of ice a mile thick, so heavy that it pressed the earth beneath it down like a thumb into wet clay. This was the Laurentide ice sheet, an unimaginably vast body that sprawled over Michigan and beyond.

The Laurentide split into four segments—the Green Bay, Lake Michigan, Erie, and Saginaw lobes.[1] And of these, the Saginaw lobe was the frailest. Precisely because it was the weakest, it would become the most influential in shaping the land that is now central Michigan. When the ice melted, it did not happen in a single graceful withdrawal. It stalled, stumbled, and pushed forward again in brief, futile surges. Each pause and push left behind a ridge of debris, like the rings of a tree marking time. Over 5,500 years, the Saginaw lobe sculpted a basin that would later funnel water into what we now call the Saginaw River.[2]

Before the ice, though, the landscape told a different tale. Michigan had been a land of rivers, a network of waterways that carved deep valleys into the earth. The glaciers, indifferent but opportunistic, followed those old paths. They widened the valleys, deepened them, and in doing so, created something entirely new: the basins of the Great Lakes.[3]

The Saginaw River exists because the land was weak enough to be reshaped by the glaciers. Fifteen thousand years ago, the world began to thaw. Slowly at first, then in fits and starts, the great ice sheets that had covered North America retreated northward.[4] The glaciers lurched backward, then forward again.

Each stumble left behind a footprint. The melting ice released torrents of water that pooled into vast, temporary lakes—proglacial lakes—occupying the low points of the land. For the first time, water began to gather in the southern Great Lakes basin. Around 15,500 years ago, an early version of Lake Huron appeared, a rough draft of the lake we know today.[5]

As the ice receded, it didn't simply reveal rivers and lakes; it reshaped them, redirected them, even reinvented them. Out of this fluid, shifting landscape, the Saginaw River began to take form—not as a single channel carved in stone, but because of convergence. The Tittabawassee and the Shiawassee, themselves molded by the glacier's restless hand, joined together and, in their union, the Saginaw River was born.

When the glaciers finally pulled back, it might seem the story concluded. Ice retreats, land clears, rivers and lakes take their place. But in truth, the drama was just beginning. The land itself had been pressed down for millennia under the unimaginable weight of a mile-thick sheet of ice. When that pressure lifted, the earth did not simply snap back. It rebounded—slowly and unevenly. Scientists call this isostatic rebound. And for thousands of years, it kept reshaping the landscape long after the ice was gone.

The effect was disorienting. Lake levels in the Great Lakes basin rose and fell by as much as sixty meters—the height of a twenty-story building.[6] These were not gentle seasonal changes. They were profound swings, dictated by shifts in climate and by the simple mechanics of drainage. A river mouth would close as land rose, only to reopen somewhere else. Lakes would shrink to near nothing, then swell again to flood their shores.

Around eight thousand years ago, a dry spell closed the Huron basin entirely. Then, just a few centuries later, increased rainfall filled it again, sending water spilling through new outlets, reworking the entire watershed—including the young, still-forming Saginaw River. In fact, the Great Lakes, as they appear on a map today, are astonishingly young. The outlines we now take for granted—Superior, Michigan, Huron, Erie, Ontario—solidified only about three thousand years ago. That is younger than the Pyramids of Egypt.

Every landscape has its quirks. In the Saginaw River watershed, one of those oddities is the kettle lake. It is just a quiet body of water, tucked into the countryside, but its origin is anything but ordinary. Each kettle lake is the ghost of an ice block, abandoned by retreating glaciers, buried in gravel and sand, and then—thousands of years later—melted into absence. What remained was not a void, but a pool of water. Something lost gave way to something new.

The glaciers left other signatures too. Along the floor of Saginaw Bay, rocky reefs rose from glacial debris. For humans, these might seem insignificant. For fish, they were perfect. Crevices between rocks sheltered eggs from predators and currents, offering not just protection, but possibility. Entire populations of native fish thrived because of a feature that existed only by accident.[7]

Over time, these quirks accumulated into something larger: a watershed that became one of the richest ecological zones in the Midwest. Rivers and wetlands braided together, supporting not just fish but also waterfowl, mammals, and plants in dazzling diversity. The Shiawassee Flats, a sprawling wetland within the watershed, emerged as a kind of ecological stage. Every year, 15 percent of the Lower Peninsula's fresh water flowed through the flats, which functioned as a filter—stripping pollutants, balancing nutrients, keeping the system in equilibrium.[8]

This was not just nature at work in isolation. The ecological foundation created by the glaciers—the kettle lakes, the reefs, the wetlands—set the stage for human life. Indigenous peoples came to the Saginaw River not simply because it was there, but because it was abundant. The river was never just a river. It was a system, an inheritance, a living archive of ice, stone, fish, and people.

The first Europeans who made their way into the Saginaw River region did not come to settle. They came to watch, to trade, to persuade. In the 1670s, a Jesuit missionary named Henri Nouvel began recording his journeys through the area. His journals are still with us—slender notes on the rivers he traveled and the people he met. But Nouvel's presence was less about geography than about purpose: The French wanted furs, and they wanted souls.

What is striking, though, is how little the French could have accomplished on their own. The waterways of Michigan—the branching creeks, the winding rivers, and the vast inland lakes—were bewildering to outsiders. For the French, the Saginaw was not a highway; it was a maze. To move through it, they had to rely almost entirely on Indigenous guides and knowledge. The very people the French hoped to convert and transform were the ones who made their presence possible.

The French influence in the Great Lakes lasted barely a century. In 1763, after the French and Indian War, France surrendered its North American possessions to Britain. Then, after the revolution, the region passed into American hands. The shifts were less about empires rising and falling, and more about the persistence of local life. Even as flags changed, trade routes and alliances remained. British influence lingered well into the War of 1812. And through it all, the Saginaw River—Indigenous long before it was European—remained what it had always been: a channel of connection, more enduring than the powers that claimed it.

The first real attempt at European settlement along the Saginaw River did not come until 1816. That year, Louis Campau set up a trading post on its banks, staking a claim in a place that had, until then, resisted permanent occupation. Trails from Detroit and Mackinac slowly opened the region to outsiders. But Campau's timing was almost audacious, because the Saginaw Valley was not, by anyone's account, an easy place to live. The river's banks were low and marshy. Seasonal flooding was a constant. Mosquitoes were everywhere. What for Indigenous peoples had been an environment to adapt to was, for newcomers, a landscape to endure.

And the reviews were brutal. Joseph Meigs, the head of the General Land Office, famously dismissed the Saginaw River as uninhabitable. "Only Indians, muskrats, and bullfrogs," he said, "could ever live on the Saginaw."[9] It was meant as sarcasm, but it reflected a broader truth: Settlers avoided the place. Compared to other parts of Michigan, where farmland looked dry and fertile, Saginaw seemed unpromising, even hostile.

Which makes its eventual development even more striking. The very features that repelled early settlers—the swamps, the floods, the mosquitoes—were precisely what had made the region ecologically rich, sustaining both wildlife and Indigenous communities for centuries. In dismissing the land, the newcomers missed the point. The Saginaw was not empty or inhospitable. It was simply a place whose value had not yet been translated into European terms.

In 1822, the U.S. government constructed Fort Saginaw, a small outpost on the Saginaw River. The fort was meant to be a symbol of authority, the physical manifestation of the United States' expanding footprint in Michigan. But almost immediately, the plan unraveled. The very landscape that had unsettled early settlers—the swamps, the stagnant water, the summer heat—turned on the soldiers themselves. Within two years, malaria had swept through the garrison with such force that the army simply gave up. The fort was abandoned, left to sink back into the marshes.

Two hundred years later, at the fort's bicentennial, people looked back with ambivalence. For some, it marked the beginning of permanent white settlement in the valley. Fort Saginaw was less a stronghold than a hinge: a brief, ill-fated experiment that nonetheless signaled the irreversible transformation of the Saginaw Valley.

The settlement of the valley began not with a rush but with a trickle. Land was surveyed, plots were drawn, and by 1835—years after the Treaty of Saginaw had opened millions of acres to white settlement—only twenty-four parcels had been sold. The rest were quietly transferred to a new developer, who tried again two years later, just in time for the Panic of 1837 to smother whatever flicker of enthusiasm remained.

It is easy, in hindsight, to imagine settlement as an unstoppable wave, the steady advance of farms, fences, and town squares. But the Saginaw Valley was different. It resisted. Flooded land, relentless mosquitoes, a financial panic two states away—each acted like a hand pushing settlers back. But sometimes history pivots on something as ordinary as a ditch filled with water. The Erie Canal, completed in 1825, was only 363 miles long and, in places, barely forty feet wide. But it collapsed distance. A farmer in Michigan could suddenly imagine his wheat, his timber, even his salted fish, on a dinner table in New York City.

In the decade after the canal opened, Michigan's white population jumped from fewer than nine thousand to nearly thirty-two thousand. Settlement was not just easier—it was suddenly inevitable. The canal, along with the modern technology of steamboats, redefined the geography of possibility. And it did not just bring settlers—it created industries.

Consider commercial fishing: Before the canal, fishing in the Great Lakes was mostly a matter of subsistence. But with an open artery eastward, fish could be salted, barreled, and sold to distant markets. By the 1830s, the American Fur Company—known for pelts—was running the first large-scale fishing operation on the Great Lakes.

What the canal demonstrates is how innovation rarely moves in straight lines. A project designed to move grain and goods ended up transforming rivers like the Saginaw into something new—not just highways of settlement, but highways of commerce, feeding industries no one had anticipated.

At first, settlement along the Saginaw River looked modest, almost tentative. A handful of cabins, a trading post, a cluster of families huddled along the east bank of the water. The river itself, wide and meandering, seemed to dwarf these early attempts at permanence. Across the bay, another community—what would become Bay City—took shape closer to where the river spilled into Lake Huron. As the population grew, county lines were redrawn, Saginaw's territory was slowly carved out of Oakland and Genesee counties, an administrative acknowledgment that something was happening here.

But what no one could quite predict was how quickly the tempo would change. By the 1830s, the valley was poised for a transformation. Clustered between the swamps and low-lying marshes was a resource that would alter the river forever: timber. White pine, stretching in vast stands across Michigan, was about to turn these tentative settlements into lumber towns of astonishing scale. Once again, the Saginaw River would serve a role of vital importance.

When the first settlers pushed into Michigan in the 1820s and 1830s, they were not met by open fields or rolling meadows. They walked into a wall of trees. Towering white pines—some more than 150 feet tall—stretched across the horizon, so dense and unbroken that to move through them was to disappear into shadow. What they saw was not just wilderness. It was potential.

The Saginaw Valley seemed almost designed for transformation. The forests here were thick and inexhaustible. And then there was the river itself: miles upon miles of branching waterways that wove through the valley, turning into a natural conveyor belt for timber. In other parts of the country, lumbermen had to solve the puzzle of how to get logs to the market. In the Saginaw, nature had already laid out the solution. It was this improbable pairing—the endless stands of pine and the perfect web of rivers—that set the stage for one of the most remarkable economic booms in Michigan's history. The settlers thought they were walking into a forest. They were walking into the raw materials of an industry.

The Saginaw Valley's lumber boom did not begin with an axe. It began with a machine. In 1834, Gardner and Ephraim Williams built a steam-powered sawmill at the foot of Mackinaw Street in Saginaw—a contraption that turned the slow, backbreaking work of cutting timber into an industrial process. It was the moment when the forests of Michigan shifted from a backdrop into big business.

Three forces converged to make Michigan's lumber economy explode.[10] The first was political: a series of treaties with the Ojibwe and other tribes that opened millions of acres of forest to white settlers. The second was demographic: settlers streaming into the vast prairies of Illinois, Iowa, Kansas, and Nebraska, where the soil was rich, but the horizon was empty of trees. They needed wood to build their homes, their barns, their towns. And the third was geography itself. Michigan's sprawling network of rivers turned out to be nature's own infrastructure, carrying logs effortlessly downstream to sawmills and, from there, out to a nation that could not get enough of the durable, versatile white pine.

When those three factors aligned, the Saginaw Valley became something larger than a place on a map. It became the engine of America's westward expansion. The Saginaw River, long a quiet artery of the landscape, was suddenly at the center of a new kind of setting. In the winter, men would cut the logs and drag them over snow to the riverbanks. When spring arrived and the ice passed, the logs moved on their own schedule, floating downstream to the sawmills that had begun to dot the river's edge.

But this was not simply a matter of brute force or luck. The industry developed an elaborate choreography, a system that turned rivers into conveyer belts on a massive scale. Cooperative boom companies organized the flow of timber. Each log carried a company mark, allowing crews to sort them at the mouths of tributaries. There, logs were assembled into floating booms, tied into rafts with rope and wedge-shaped oak pins—a technique the Saginaw

River became famous for.[11] Wooden pins held together thousands of pounds of timber, a fragile yet brilliant solution to a monumental logistical challenge. The result was efficiency on a scale that seems almost impossible today. Logs traveled from inland forests to riverfront sawmills, where they were processed into lumber for homes, barns, and towns far beyond Michigan. By 1854, the Saginaw Valley was the state's leading producer of lumber, a distinction it would hold for the next forty years. By 1869, the watershed alone was generating $7 million a year. Michigan, it seemed, had discovered a natural monopoly: more lumber than any other state in the nation, flowing from the Saginaw River to a growing Midwest.[12]

The secret was not just the trees. It was technology. Sawmills had begun to evolve from simple contraptions into machines of astonishing efficiency. Blades were refined. Gang saws were introduced. By 1882, these innovations transformed potential into reality: the Saginaw Valley alone yielded a billion board feet of lumber in a single year.[13] And then, at the peak in 1889–1890, the scale became almost incomprehensible. Michigan produced 5.5 billion board feet of lumber—roughly ten times the amount produced in a modern year.[14] Most of it was pine, harvested, transported, and processed in a way dictated by rivers, machines, and human labor.

The lumber industry did not just harvest trees—it built towns. Along the Saginaw River, the first sawmills acted like magnets, drawing people, commerce, and ambition to the banks. Boarding houses went up for workers, shops opened for residents, and suddenly, small settlements that had seemed permanent in their modesty were transformed into bustling industrial hubs. Saginaw and Bay City emerged as the clear centers of this new world. Their growth was not accidental. Every board cut and every raft floated downstream created jobs, pulled in immigrants, and spun off new businesses. Blacksmiths, merchants, carpenters—an entire ecosystem of labor and commerce rose in the shadow of the timber. Roads, bridges, and docks followed the logs, creating infrastructure that made the towns permanent, even after the forests themselves were gone.

The Saginaw Valley economic narrative only began to get interesting when the region discovered that the trees it was cutting could do double duty.[15] By the late 1850s, the East Saginaw Salt Manufacturing Company had figured out something remarkable: The waste from sawmills—the bark, the slabs, the scraps that had no other use—could be burned to fuel the evaporation of brine into salt. Timber became both a product and power source, and suddenly two industries were intertwined.

Michigan's first successful commercial salt operation opened in 1859, and it did not take long for production in the region to explode. By 1888, the state boasted 127 salt companies producing 5.2 million barrels a year—nearly half of the nation's supply.[16] What's fascinating is not just the scale, but the way the salt and lumber industries fed each other. Lumbering created both the raw materials and the energy for salt production, while salt added a new layer of economic value to the region that had once seemed to rely solely on timber.

The same forests that had transformed the Saginaw Valley into an industrial hub for lumber also became the hidden engine for another booming enterprise. The constructive interaction of wood and brine turned the valley into a kind of laboratory for resource maximization—a place where the accidents of geography and industry produced outcomes that no one had fully anticipated.

By the mid-nineteenth century, the Saginaw River had become more than a waterway—it was a conveyor belt, a lifeline, and the stage for a new kind of industry: shipbuilding. Lumber could be cut, milled, and stacked on the riverbanks, but there was a problem: It had to reach the growing towns and cities of the lower Great Lakes. The solution was inevitable. If the trees could not walk, someone would build ships to carry them.

And so, the Saginaw River became a shipyard. Vessels were designed specifically for lumber transport, sturdy and capacious, built for one purpose: to move the valley's timber wealth across water. In 1876, Frank W. Wheeler—a captain, a builder, and eventually a politician—opened the West Bay City Shipbuilding Company, later renamed the F. W. Wheeler Company. It sat on the river near Third Street, a reminder that industrial innovation often grows organically out of necessity. Shipbuilding became a pillar of the local economy, complementing lumber while giving the river a new significance. The Saginaw River was no longer just a route through the landscape—it was a hub, a connector, a mechanism through which inland resources reached distant markets.

By the early twentieth century, the forests that had defined the Saginaw River watershed were gone. Clear-cutting was so thorough that by 1910, the towering white pines and dense hardwood that once blanketed the region had all but vanished. The consequences were immediate and visible. Without trees catching rainfall, the land could no longer absorb water or anchor soil. Rain that once seeped slowly into the ground now rushed unchecked into rivers, carrying sediment and debris, and reshaping the very flow of the Saginaw. What had been a predictable, stable river system became erratic, muddied, and strained under the weight of human activity.

The era of Saginaw lumbering had ended, leaving behind not just empty mills and depleted fortunes, but a watershed fundamentally altered—a reminder that human ingenuity, when paired with natural abundance, can create both prosperity and destruction. The consequences rippled outward. Industries built on lumber, salt production chief among them, collapsed almost as quickly as the trees fell. Without sawdust and other mill waste to fuel evaporation, many salt operations became uneconomical. "When the lumber was gone, and the lumber towns vanished, the salt industry vanished with them," one historian noted, "but only in the vanished towns."[17] In other words, the fortunes of an entire region had been inseparably linked to a single natural resource.

Yet this was not an end, only a pivot. Communities along the Saginaw River had been shaped by lumber, but they were not defined by it. As the forests disappeared, the communities that remained turned to new industries, continuing a lengthy process of transformation that had begun with settlers, rivers, and innovation. The Saginaw River, once simply a natural waterway, had become an industrial corridor—and even as one era closed, the river itself remained, carrying the next chapter of economic life.

When the lumber era ended, the Saginaw River communities faced a question that is as old as economic history itself: What comes after the boom? The forests were gone, the mills were silent, and yet the infrastructure—the roads, the river channels, the towns themselves—remained. In the spaces left by fallen pines, opportunity quietly waited.

Enter Herbert H. Dow. In 1890, he arrived in Midland, a town on the Tittabawassee River (one of the Saginaw's major tributaries), and he saw potential where others saw exhausted wells.[18] Using brine that had long been a source of salt, Dow pioneered a method to extract chemicals—chlorine in particular—that transformed a simple, nearly forgotten industry into a sophisticated chemical enterprise. By redeveloping an 1870 brine well, he demonstrated that chemical extraction from brine was not just possible, but profitable.

Dow's innovation did more than create a company. It turned Midland, and the broader Saginaw watershed, into the birthplace of a new industrial era. What had been a modest salt operation became a high-tech chemical industry with enormous economic and environmental consequences. The river that had once carried logs now carried chemicals, marking the next chapter in the evolution of the region. From lumber to salt to chemistry, each era layered atop the last, building on the infrastructure and ingenuity left behind by those who had come before. As Michigan's automotive revolution took hold in Detroit and spread, manufacturing facilities sprang up along the river, turning towns like Saginaw into producers of components for a burgeoning national phenomenon. The region was no longer defined solely by natural resources, it was now defined by its capacity to transform them into machines, parts, and, eventually, weapons.

World War I marked the first test of this industrial agility. In January 1918, the Saginaw Shipbuilding Company began producing canal-size ocean freight ships for the U.S. Army Supply Service. At its peak, the company employed over 500 mechanics and laborers, a number that swelled to 1,800 at full production. The river, once a highway for logs, had become a conveyor belt for steel, labor, and ingenuity.

World War II accelerated the transformation. Saginaw's factories shifted to meet the demands of war—producing munitions, vehicle components, and even rifles. One facility alone turned out more than half a million M1 carbines for the U.S. military. The river towns, shaped centuries earlier by forests and brine, had evolved into a hub of national importance. What had begun as a landscape defined by natural abundance was now a landscape defined by human innovation, adaptability, and the relentless capacity to meet the moment.

Rivers in their natural state are rarely ready for the ambitions of industry. By the twentieth century, the Saginaw River had become more than a historical route for logs or a convenient waterway for early mills—it was poised to become a major commercial artery. But to fulfill that potential, it needed to be reshaped.

Between 1910 and 1965, a series of federal Rivers and Harbors Acts authorized a remarkable engineering project.[19] The goal was deceptively simple: make the river navigable for the growing fleets of commercial vessels that now defined the region's economy. The result, however, was anything but simple. The Saginaw River was sculpted into a sophisticated channel with depths and widths varying to accommodate different types of ships, from the 27-foot-wide entrance at Saginaw Bay to the 16.5-foot stretch upstream at Green Point. Five turning basins were added, carefully designed to allow vessels to maneuver with precision.[20]

These modifications did more than facilitate shipping. They transformed the river itself into a machine of commerce, a deliberate conduit for industrial growth. Factories, warehouses, and ports along its banks could now count on reliable access to national and international markets. The river—once a natural landscape—had become a carefully calibrated tool, reshaped to carry the ambitions of the communities and industries that had grown up around it. By the mid-twentieth century, the Saginaw River had quietly become a commercial corridor connecting the heart of Michigan to the farthest reaches of the Great Lakes—and, in three days, to the Atlantic Ocean. What makes the river extraordinary is not its size, but this connectivity. The shipping channel links local ports to the St. Lawrence Seaway, transforming a regional economy into a participant in global trade. It is a reminder that geography alone is rarely enough; what matters is the infrastructure that amplifies it, the deliberate human effort to turn a river into a conduit for opportunity.

Saginaw County exemplifies this principle. Highways, railroads, an international airport, and multiple port facilities all intersect with the river, creating an intermodal network that allows goods—and ideas—to move seamlessly from local factories to international markets. The Saginaw River, once a natural landscape shaped by glaciers, then timber, now carries commerce on a scale its earliest settlers could scarcely imagine. It is not just a river. It is the lifeline of an economy, a quiet engine powering the region's connection to the world.

It is easy to think of rivers as relics of another era, symbols of a time when industry was powered by water rather than silicon. But the river defies that narrative. It continues to do what it has always done, connecting places, moving goods, and shaping the fortunes of the cities along its banks. It was for this reason—commerce—that in the quiet, early hours of September 16, 1990, the *Jupiter*, a 392-foot-long tanker, made its way up the Saginaw River, arriving at the Total Petroleum terminal near Bay City. It was an arrival like countless others before it, the latest link in a supply chain that stretched across international waters.

The *Jupiter* had set out the day before from Sarnia, Ontario, its massive tanks filled with fifty-four thousand barrels of unleaded gasoline—more than 2.3

million gallons of fuel, enough to power a small city.[21] It had traveled across the smooth, glassy expanse of Lake Huron, slipping past the familiar landmarks of the Great Lakes shipping lanes, heading inland toward mid-Michigan, on a routine trip it had done dozens of times before.

The *Jupiter*, constructed in 1976 by S. B. A. Shipyards in Jennings, Louisiana, was designed to move chemicals efficiently and safely—a workhorse of the industrial supply chain.[22] Commissioned by Cleveland Tankers a subsidiary of Ashland Petroleum Company, it was not a particularly remarkable vessel. But beneath its steel exterior was a system engineered for precision. Its propulsion came from two General Motors diesel engines, connected through reduction gears to stainless steel propellers. A bridge control system allowed the engines to be operated directly from the wheelhouse, a feature that spoke to the growing sophistication of maritime technology. Power was supplied by three 300-kilowatt diesel generators, ensuring that even in the middle of the Great Lakes, the ship functioned like a self-contained city.[23]

Life on board followed the rhythms of the ship. Crew quarters were divided along the port and starboard sides of the main deck, with a galley and messroom at the center—functional, efficient, a floating home for the men who worked the vessel. Above them, the wheelhouse stood like a command center, offering an unobstructed view over the bow and reinforcing the idea that a ship, no matter how large, is only as good as the people guiding it.

Beneath the deck, the *Jupiter* was a study in balance and control. Its cargo section was divided into twelve tanks—six on each side—separated by bulkheads and linked by a network of pipelines, valves, and electric deep well pumps designed to move cargo with the precision of a surgical instrument.[24] A separate ballast system, with its own dedicated pump, ensured that the vessel remained level in the water, adjusting for the shifting weight of its liquid cargo. Even spilled product was accounted for: Six-inch steel containment rails lined the deck, preventing any overflow from escaping into open water.

The ship carried three twenty-person life rafts, twenty-four life jackets, twenty-three immersion suits, and a full array of emergency gear, from fire hoses and extinguishers to a fixed-foam extinguishing system positioned to smother flames before they could take hold.[25] The engine room, the heart of the vessel, was protected by a fixed halon system, an invisible safeguard in a space where a single spark could mean disaster.

The *Jupiter* was built to move. It was built to endure. But the thing about machines—no matter how well-designed—is that they exist in a world where control is never absolute. And sometimes, even the most meticulously engineered systems meet forces they were never meant to withstand.

As the *Jupiter* unloaded its cargo on that chilly September morning, another ship, the *Buffalo*, began up the Saginaw River, having come from Lake Huron. The *Buffalo* was not the biggest ship on the Great Lakes—not by a long shot. At 634 feet, it was impressive, but in a world where 1,000-foot freighters ruled the waterways, it was a mid-sized player. What made it stand out, however, was not its size but its purpose. Built in 1978 by Bay Shipbuilding Corporation in Sturgeon Bay, Wisconsin, it was designed to do one thing exceptionally well: move cargo efficiently.[26]

Named after Buffalo, New York—the home of its original owner, the American Steamship Company—the *Buffalo* was a self-unloading bulk carrier, built for speed and practicality. Its propulsion system was built around two General Motors B-20-645-E7 diesel engines, connected through reduction gears to a single stainless-steel controllable-pitch propeller.[27] From the bridge, the crew had full control over the ship's movement, aided by bow and stern thrusters that made maneuvering a vessel of this scale surprisingly precise.

But the real genius of *Buffalo* was in its cargo handling system. Below deck, five massive cargo holds—ranging from 72 to 120 feet in length—were fed by twenty hatches.[28] Unloading was a seamless process: Twin conveyor belts moved bulk materials along the length of the ship, transferring them to a 220-foot discharge boom that could quickly deposit coal, limestone, or grain onto waiting docks. And when the holds were empty, the *Buffalo* carried something else: 14,154 tons of water ballast, stored in twelve double-bottom tanks, ensuring that the ship remained stable even without a heavy load.

Life aboard the *Buffalo* revolved around its single deckhouse, positioned just aft of the engine room. It was here that the crew ate, slept, and worked, housed alongside the ship's navigating bridge and conveyor machinery. Safety was an ever-present concern, and the *Buffalo* was well-equipped: a thirty-person lifeboat, four inflatable life rafts, thirty-six life jackets, thirty-two immersion suits, and enough fire suppression equipment to manage nearly any emergency.[29] In the engine room, a fixed halon fire suppression system stood guard, while a carbon-dioxide system protected the emergency generator room—a testament to the understanding that, on the water, disaster was always a possibility.

By the time September 1990 arrived, the *Buffalo* had already passed through multiple owners. The American Steamship Company sold it to Lawrence

Steamship Company in 1983, and then in 1989, ownership transferred again—this time to Connecticut Bank and Trust. Ships change hands all the time, shuffling between corporations and financial institutions, but what doesn't change is their purpose. The *Buffalo* was built to move, and no matter who owned it, that's exactly what it continued to do.

Bay City sits just two miles from where the Saginaw River spills into Saginaw Bay, a city built around the water, shaped by its ebb and flow. In 1819, a man named Stephan Riley received the first registered land grant in what would one day be Bay County, Michigan.[30] But a piece of paper is not a community, and Riley's claim, like so many early ventures into the frontier, didn't signal permanence. Real settlement came a dozen years later, in 1831, when Leon Tromblé—a Frenchman from Detroit—arrived with an unusual mission: to teach Native Americans how to farm.

Tromblé built a rough-hewn log cabin on the east bank of the Saginaw River and, in doing so, became the area's first colonizer. A few years later, in 1834, another man, John B. Trudell, followed, putting up his own cabin just downriver. Trudell wasn't passing through; he stayed. The decision to remain rather than move on is why he is remembered as the county's first permanent resident. For the better part of a decade, though, the tiny community amounted to little more than a trading post. Europeans were present, but barely.

The river, however, was destiny. The Saginaw flowed deeper here than it did in the neighboring settlements, deep enough for big ships. In the age before railroads stitched the country's interior together, that single fact—depth—was everything. It meant lumber and goods could move in bulk. It meant growth.

At first, the place was called "Lower Saginaw," a name that acknowledged its geography and its dependency on the larger town upriver. It wasn't until June 4, 1846, with the opening of the Hampton Post Office, that Lower Saginaw truly began to stand on its own. A post office is a small, bureaucratic detail, but in the nineteenth century it was a marker of legitimacy. A community with mail service was no longer just a scatter of cabins; it was a place on the map.

In the winter of 1855, a man named Jonathan Smith Barclay—Saginaw's representative in the state legislature—took up a cause that seemed, at first glance, to be almost procedural. He wanted to carve a new county out of the old one. With the quiet backing of Albert Miller and Daniel Burns, Barclay introduced a bill to create Bay County. It failed by just a handful of votes.

But failure in politics is often temporary. Two years later, despite the predictable opposition of neighboring counties that stood to lose influence, the measure passed. On February 17, 1857, Bay County was born. That bureaucratic shift was more than lines on a map. It was a declaration of independence. And independence, in nineteenth-century America, demanded a new identity. "Lower Saginaw" no longer fit. It was too derivative, too tethered to the town upriver. So, in 1858, the post office formally embraced a new name: Bay City.

Names matter. They are both practical and aspirational. "Bay City" said something about geography—anchoring the community on the waters of Saginaw Bay—but it also carried a subtle ambition. It sounded larger, sturdier, more permanent. To call itself a "city," even when it was little more than a cluster of streets and storefronts, was to imagine a future of consequence. And in the mid-nineteenth century, imagination often came before reality.

By 1860, what had once been the modest outpost of Lower Saginaw was no longer modest. Two thousand people lived there now, drawn by mills and small shops that clustered along the riverbank. The timing mattered. The American Civil War, which broke out the following year, coincided with the community's first true surge of growth. Conflict in Washington meant opportunity in Michigan.

In 1865, the settlement made a declaration that went beyond population counts. It incorporated. With a population of just 3,359, Bay City legally severed itself from the townships of Hampton and Portsmouth, and drafted its own charter.[31] A few years earlier, in 1859, the villagers had held their first election—Curtis Munger was chosen as village president—but incorporation was different. Incorporation was permanence.

The gamble paid off. In a single decade, Bay City's population nearly tripled, rising from 7,064 in 1870 to more than 20,000 by 1880.[32] The reason was obvious to anyone who stood on the riverbank and watched the lumber barges drift past. The lumber industry was booming, and with it came laborers, traders, and entrepreneurs from across the United States and Europe. The city was no longer a frontier outpost. It was an economic magnet.

The transformation required institutions. In 1858, the county's first courthouse—a simple wooden structure on Water Street—had been rented for $200 a year. That humble courthouse quickly became insufficient. By 1867, the county's population had jumped from just 700 people eight years earlier to more than 15,000. Growth demanded governance, and governance demanded infrastructure.

And then, in 1905, the city made another leap. East Bay City and West Bay City—two municipalities divided by the Saginaw River and divided, too, by competing loyalties—consolidated into one. The merger was practical, but it was also symbolic. It signaled that Bay City was no longer simply a collection of neighborhoods and mills strung along a river. It was a regional power in its own right, unified and competitive.

In 1905, a young boatbuilder named Harry J. Defoe set up shop on the banks of the Saginaw River.[33] His enterprise was modest: He built what were called "knock-down" boats—flat-packed vessels shipped in pieces and assembled elsewhere—and a few gasoline-powered craft for businessmen and weekend pleasure seekers. Bay City had once been a lumber town, and in the aftermath of that boom, small ventures like Defoe's seemed almost quaint, a way of keeping the river useful.

But Defoe's company didn't stay small for long. What began as a wooden boat shop grew into one of America's great shipyards, a place that would eventually turn out sleek naval warships and support craft for navies around the world. The transformation wasn't simply about scale; it was about invention.

Defoe engineers pioneered something they called the "upside-down and roll-over" method. It was a simple, almost playful idea: build the hull upside down, so the welding could be done "hand down," with gravity in your favor. When the hull was finished, enormous wheels at either end flipped the ship over. It was efficient, elegant, and, most of all, faster. During World War II, that mattered. Between 1939 and 1945, Defoe's firm produced 154 ships—minesweepers, destroyer escorts, patrol craft, landing craft. The U.S. Navy awarded the yard its coveted "E" for excellence six times, a testament to how an idea born out of practicality had reshaped industrial production.

After the war, the shipyard adapted again. It built Great Lakes freighters, carried out conversions and repairs, and even produced guided missile destroyers for both the U.S. Navy and the Royal Australian Navy. The craftsmanship was so refined that the White House came calling: Defoe built John F. Kennedy's yacht, the *Honey Fitz*, a vessel that was part leisure, part political stage.

And yet, like so many great industrial stories, the arc ended not with triumph but with silence. In the mid-1970s, as the Vietnam War wound down, the navy chose not to renew its contracts. Without the steady hum of government orders, the shipyard that had once symbolized American ingenuity had no future. On December 31, 1975, after seventy years, the Defoe Shipbuilding Company shut its doors. That is the paradox of innovation. A company born in improvisation, made great by efficiency, and remembered for excellence was ultimately undone by forces far beyond its control.

When Bay City's lumber era faded, the assumption was that the town's best days were behind it. Lumber towns, after all, rarely survived the exhaustion of the forests that sustained them. And yet, by the 1920s, Bay City had quietly rewritten its destiny. The future wasn't in trees anymore—it was in machines.

One company symbolized this shift better than any other: the Industrial Works, later known as Industrial Brownhoist.[34] By 1928, it employed 850 men, an enormous number considering the city's size. The Fraser family, who founded the company in 1873, specialized in an odd but essential technology: rail-mounted shovels and cranes. Their machines weren't just tools of industry; they were emblems of modern ambition. A Brownhoist crane towered over the 1893 Chicago Columbian Exposition, an icon of America's industrial might. A decade later, another would help dig the Panama Canal, an engineering marvel that redefined global trade.

And then came General Motors. In 1918, GM planted itself firmly in the region, establishing the Saginaw Metal Castings Operations (once known as Grey Iron).[35] The foundry became indispensable to GM's production network, and when World War II erupted, part of the foundry pivoted almost overnight to producing magnesium for Pratt and Whitney airplane engines. What had once fueled cars now fueled fighter planes.

Bay City's industrial story wasn't just about scale; it was about diversity. The General Cigar Company, for instance, employed three hundred people at its South Madison Avenue plant in the late 1920s and would have hired more if only the city could supply the skilled hands.[36] Manufacturing here wasn't dominated by one product or one company—it was a mosaic of industries, each threading the city more tightly into the fabric of twentieth-century America.

Bay City has always lived with fire. It is the kind of risk that comes with wooden buildings, overburdened wiring, and the dense clusters of activity that define an industrial town. The Wenonah Hotel fire was Bay City's darkest night.[37] On December 10, 1977, faulty wiring ignited an inferno that spread faster than residents could react. More than 140 people were inside when the flames erupted.

Some jumped from third- and fourth-story windows. Ten people didn't survive. Dozens more were injured. And what made the loss worse was that the Wenonah wasn't just a hotel. It was the city's living room, a place where neighbors gathered for celebrations and banquets, where ordinary life intersected with civic pride. Its destruction was not just physical; it was cultural.

If fire was Bay City's recurring enemy within, water was its threat from without. The Saginaw River made the city prosperous, but it also made it vulnerable. The most catastrophic reminder of that vulnerability came in 1986, when a rare weather pattern known as "train-echoing" stalled a cluster of storm systems over Michigan. The result was relentless rain—so much of it that thirty counties were declared disaster zones.

Bay City was at the center of the disaster. The Great Flood of 1986 caused half a billion dollars in damage, the equivalent of more than a billion dollars today.[38] The agricultural toll was devastating, with half the dry beans in Midland County gone, nearly a third of Saginaw's crops destroyed, and even higher losses in Tuscola and Gratiot Counties. A meteorological quirk had undone a year's worth of labor.

Taken together, these disasters tell us something about the paradox of place. The very features that made Bay City thrive—its dense urban structures, its riverfront location, its role as a regional hub—were the same features that left it vulnerable. Prosperity and peril, it turns out, are often two sides of the same coin.

On paper, the stretch of river where the Total Petroleum terminal sat belongs to Bangor Township, but in practice the distinction is almost meaningless. To the people who live and work here, borders are secondary to the river itself. Do you live on the east side or the west? The water, not the lines on a map, defines the land.

The Saginaw River is lined on both banks with wharves, docks, and industrial facilities that have long distinguished the region's economy. About 6.5 miles from the river's mouth sits the Midland Contracting Company pier, one of the many stops for freighters like the *Buffalo*, which navigate these waters with precision, carrying the raw materials that keep the region moving. Bay City and Saginaw's port area is not built for spectacle; it's built for commerce. Petroleum products, grain, limestone, coal, sand, gravel, cement—this is the language of industry, the quiet machinery of trade that flows in and out of the river every day. It is also a designated customs port of entry, a reminder that while the Saginaw River may feel local, its connections stretch far beyond mid-Michigan. This is a place where industry and infrastructure meet, and where the work of the Great Lakes continues, unnoticed by most but essential all the same.

In September 1990, a survey by the U.S. Army Corps of Engineers captured a snapshot of the Saginaw River's depths—a precise measurement of a landscape in constant motion.[39] Opposite the Total Petroleum berth, the dredged channel plunged to 26.8 feet at mean low water, a depth carefully engineered to accommodate the steady flow of industry. But at the pier itself, the river was less predictable. Here, the depth wavered between 24 and 26 feet, a subtle but significant variation that could mean the difference between smooth passage and an unexpected complication. These numbers, dry and technical on the surface, hint at a larger truth: Rivers are never truly static. They shift and settle, responding to forces both natural and manufactured, reshaping themselves moment by moment—even as we try to measure them.

The morning of September 16, the *Buffalo* moved steadily up the river, its steel hull slicing through calm waters, a light breeze whispering against its frame. The air sat just above 50 degrees—a brisk but unremarkable start to the day. Overhead, an approaching weather system gathered strength, preparing to drape the river in sheets of relentless rain. Onboard, the crew went about their routine, unaware what they were stepping into.

In the world of maritime travel, fate rarely announces itself. Instead, it arrives in the form of a sequence—small, inconsequential moments that, when strung together, create something irreversible. And so, as the *Buffalo* pressed forward, the pieces aligned. Before the day passed, this vessel and another—the *Jupiter*—would be forever entwined, their names linked in a narrative shaped not by chance, but by the precise and unyielding mechanics of cause and effect.

Chapter 2

When Hell Visited the Saginaw River

JUST BEFORE 7 A.M., THE WORLD WAS STILL CLOAKED IN DARKNESS AS THE BULK carrier *Buffalo* eased into the channel leading to the Saginaw River. It was a routine passage, the kind of journey the freighter had made countless times before. Onboard, over thirteen thousand tons of coal sat in its hold, bound for the Midland Contracting pier farther upriver.[1]

At the helm stood Captain John MacFalda, forty-two years old, guiding the vessel with the practiced confidence of a seasoned mariner. But MacFalda wasn't *Buffalo*'s usual captain—he was filling in, stepping into a role that was not quite his own, occupying a seat meant for someone else, who at that moment was miles away, on vacation.[2] The crew in the pilothouse that morning—comprised of the master, the first mate, and the wheelsman—moved through the familiar rhythms of a morning transit. Everything appeared ordinary. And yet, as the *Buffalo* pushed forward, it was unknowingly heading toward a moment that would make this voyage anything but routine.

MacFalda was not a novice.[3] He was, by every measure, a seasoned mariner, someone who had spent decades mastering the intricate dance of ship and water. Holding a Coast Guard license as both a master and first-class pilot for vessels of any cargo type, MacFalda had built a career on precision and expertise. Since 1971, he had been with the American Steamship Company, the owner of the *Buffalo*, and by 1982, he had risen to the rank of master, commanding massive one-thousand-foot freighters with the ease that only experience allows.

MacFalda's navigational footprint stretched beyond the Great Lakes, reaching as far as Port Revell, France, a testament to the breadth of his maritime knowledge. And while his time aboard the *Buffalo* was limited, the Saginaw River was no mystery to him. That year alone, he had made the trip five times—enough to know its curves, its depths, and the subtleties of its current.

At around 7 a.m., the first mate of the *Buffalo* reached for the ship's radio and made a routine security broadcast—a simple but essential message, alerting nearby vessels that they were making their way up the Saginaw River.[4] It was the kind of transmission that happened countless times a day, the background hum of maritime life, unnoticed until something went wrong. Moments later, he placed another call, this time to the Coast Guard station, requesting a tide reading. The response came back: a 33-inch rise. A small but significant detail.

The *Buffalo*, heavy with coal, rode low in the water—15 feet, 6 inches at the bow, nearly 19 feet at the stern.[5] These numbers mattered. They dictated how the ship would move, how it would respond to currents and obstacles, how much room—if any—existed between its hull and the riverbed below. In the world of Great Lakes shipping, the margins are everything. A few inches of clearance can mean the difference between a smooth passage and a costly miscalculation. And as the *Buffalo* pushed forward, those inches would soon become more important than anyone on board could have imagined.

At 7:30 a.m., Richard P. Hollingsworth stepped in to take over the watch.[6] At thirty-five years old, he was new to the *Buffalo*—this was his first season aboard—but he was hardly inexperienced. A seasoned mariner with a Coast Guard license as both a mate and first-class pilot, Hollingsworth had spent years navigating Great Lakes freighters, developing the instincts that come only with time on the water.[7] The Saginaw River was familiar territory. That season alone, he had sailed it roughly twenty times, enough to know its quirks—the bends that demanded a steady hand, the invisible forces that could nudge a vessel off course. Still, experience, even in repetition, has its limits. The river is never the same twice.

By 8 a.m., the *Buffalo* was making good time, cutting through the water at a steady eleven to twelve knots. At that speed, the ship moved with confidence, a steel giant gliding toward its destination. But as it reached buoys 27 and 28—the unofficial gateway to the Saginaw River—momentum gave way to caution.[8] The throttle eased back, slowing the vessel to six or seven knots, a necessary adjustment for what lay ahead.

The river narrowed, its margins tightening around the *Buffalo* as it pressed forward. At the helm, Captain MacFalda keyed the radio once more, sending out another security broadcast.[9] It was a standard call, a brief declaration of presence and intent—one ship making its position known in a waterway shared by many. But shipping is a world where small moments accumulate, where a routine message, a shift in speed, or a minor adjustment in course can quietly shape the future. And as the *Buffalo* moved deeper into the river, the stage was being set for something no one could yet see.

As the *Buffalo* approached the Detroit and Mackinac (D&M) railroad bridge, Captain MacFalda took in the scene ahead: a ship moored along the west side of the river, an obstacle that required subtle but deliberate adjustment. With years of experience guiding freighters through tight passages, he made a small but calculated shift, steering the *Buffalo* toward the right-hand opening of the bridge. It was no ordinary bridge: Unlike the towering lift bridges that rise to accommodate passing vessels, this one swung open horizontally, pivoting like a massive door on the river.

Dr. George Ascherl Jr. was a man who understood the water. Aboard his forty-foot sailboat, *Wild Irish*, he had been idling at the pier of the Saginaw Bay Yacht Club, a mere quarter mile upstream from the Coast Guard station. The moment was quiet, anticipatory—until the *Buffalo* passed.[10] Then, Ascherl made his move. With the precision of a seasoned mariner, he eased *Wild Irish* into the river, positioning himself roughly three hundred feet astern of the larger vessel. The two ships, disparate in scale but momentarily linked by circumstance, threaded their way toward the D&M railroad bridge. The water, ever indifferent to the plans of men, carried them forward.

As the *Buffalo* pressed forward, carving its path upriver, it let out a resonant whistle—a coded request understood by those who knew these waters well. It was calling for the raising of the Independence Bridge, the first of Bay City's four bascule bridges, a steel sentinel standing between the ship and its destination. Navigating a river like this wasn't just a matter of steering; it was a negotiation, a careful balance between power and precision. The *Buffalo* aimed deliberately for the right-hand pier, holding its position in the center of the channel.

At 1:45 a.m., under the cover of darkness, the 392-foot tankship *Jupiter* had made its quiet arrival at the Total Petroleum facility, a point along the river about a mile and a half upstream from Bay City.[11] It had traveled through the night, departing from a refinery in Sarnia, Canada. Onboard were fifty-six thousand barrels of unleaded gasoline, a commodity so ubiquitous that few people ever stopped to consider the intricate choreography required to move it from one place to another. Now, at this late hour, the *Jupiter* prepared for the final step in its journey: the careful discharge of its cargo at the Total Petroleum terminal, another link in the vast, unseen network that powered daily life.

The story of gasoline began in 1851, when Henry and Charles Tripp arrived at what is now Oil Springs, Ontario, drawn by rumors of "gum beds" along the Dundee limestone formation—part of the same Michigan Basin that stretches across state lines.[12] They drilled, they experimented, and in doing so, they tapped into a resource that would redefine the modern world. It's a detail often overlooked: The world's first commercial oil development occurred here, before Edwin Drake sank his famous well in Pennsylvania. As the Clarke Historical Library at Central Michigan University wryly notes, "If Michigan could borrow twenty miles of Canada, it could lay claim to being the cradle of the worldwide oil industry."[13] A small geographic quirk, a mere stretch of border, shifts the narrative of an entire global industry.

Underlying this human story is a geological one. The Michigan Basin, a bowl-shaped remnant of an ancient tropical sea, holds layer upon layer of sedimentary rock, millions of years in the making. This natural formation, extending from the Upper Peninsula down to Ohio and from Niagara Falls to Wisconsin, created perfect conditions for oil and gas to accumulate. Without it, the Tripp brothers' gamble might never have paid off. What seems like a simple discovery—a few gushes of oil from a sandy bed—was actually the result of eons of geological fortune meeting human curiosity and enterprise.

The transformation of oil from a curiosity into a pillar of the American economy didn't happen in a single leap. It began quietly, in Cleveland, Ohio, in 1863, when a young John D. Rockefeller partnered with M. B. Clark and chemist Samuel Andrews to form Andrews, Clark, and Company, an oil refining business.[14] By 1865, Rockefeller and Andrews had bought out Clark's share, creating Rockefeller and Andrews—a modest enterprise that would soon become a juggernaut.

Cleveland at the time was not yet synonymous with petroleum, but it had the ingredients Rockefeller needed: proximity to crude oil supplies in Pennsylvania and Ohio, an intricate network of railroads, and a port on Lake Erie that could move refined oil with unprecedented efficiency. "Rockefeller took advantage of Cleveland's many railroads to bring crude oil from Pennsylvania and western Ohio to his refineries," notes Teaching Cleveland Digital.[15] It was a lesson in seeing opportunity not just in resources, but in the infrastructure connecting them.

By January 10, 1870, Rockefeller formally established Standard Oil. At that moment, the company controlled a modest 10 percent of U.S. oil production. What followed was a master class in industrial strategy. Through acquisitions, operational efficiencies, and aggressive—sometimes ruthless—business practices, Rockefeller consolidated control. The infamous "Cleveland Massacre" of 1872 was a turning point: Local competitors were bought out or pushed aside, clearing the way for a near-monopoly. By 1879, a mere fourteen years after founding Standard Oil, Rockefeller controlled 90 percent of American oil production.[16]

Cleveland, in turn, was transformed. Standard Oil employed thousands, generated immense wealth, and anchored the city's economy even through crises like the Panic of 1873. The city's fortunes were now inseparable from Rockefeller's vision. What had begun as a small refinery along Lake Erie became the epicenter of the nation's petroleum industry, illustrating how strategic insight, timing, and infrastructure can elevate a single enterprise into a force that reshapes both an industry and a city.

John D. Rockefeller's methods were controversial, but they were also brilliant. He understood something fundamental about business long before many of his contemporaries: Efficiency is power. By securing favorable railroad rebates, Standard Oil could transport its oil at lower costs than competitors, undercutting prices and quietly tightening its grip on the market. What looked like ruthless strategy was, in fact, a calculated exploitation of infrastructure—a lesson in how control over logistics can be as decisive as control over resources.

In 1882, Rockefeller took this vision one step further, creating the Standard Oil Trust. This was not just a company; it was a new kind of business structure, one designed to consolidate control in ways that were nearly invisible to outsiders. Nine trustees, including Rockefeller himself, oversaw a network that eventually encompassed forty corporations, fourteen of them wholly owned by Standard Oil.

Even after the State of Ohio dissolved the trust in 1892, Standard Oil's dominance did not waver. It continued to shape the industry until its eventual breakup in 1911. Rockefeller had created something more enduring than a company: It was a blueprint for vertical integration, a model of corporate power that would influence generations of business leaders. In his hands, oil was more than a commodity; it was a lesson in strategy, patience, and the quiet, relentless accumulation of control.

In the early days of the oil industry, refineries weren't producing what we now think of as the lifeblood of modern transportation. Their focus was kerosene, a clean-burning liquid that had replaced whale oil as the preferred source of light. By 1866, Cleveland refineries were shipping most of this kerosene to Europe, tapping into what had become the world's most lucrative market. The industry's early fortunes were built on illumination, not gasoline.

Gasoline, by contrast, was a curiosity, even a nuisance. It was dangerous, volatile, and of little apparent value. Newspaper accounts of the time noted that it was "the least desirable" product of refinement—so undesirable, in fact, that it was routinely siphoned off into the Cuyahoga River, where it occasionally caught fire.[17] In hindsight, this casual disposal seems reckless. Yet it is also revealing: The very by-product that would fuel the twentieth century's transportation revolution was once treated as waste. This early period illustrates a paradox at the heart of industrial progress: The most transformative innovations often emerge from what is initially overlooked or undervalued. And it foreshadows another, darker legacy—how the pursuit of profit and efficiency would increasingly intersect with environmental consequences, for the Great Lakes and beyond.

War has a way of reshaping industries, often in ways no one anticipates. In the Great Lakes region, the two world wars were precisely that kind of catalyst for the petrochemical industry. During World War II, the stakes were global, and the demand for innovation was urgent. On the Canadian side, the Sarnia area—what would eventually earn the moniker "Chemical Valley"—emerged as a strategic linchpin.[18] There, factories churned out synthetic rubber for the Allied forces, a product so vital that it became central to tanks, trucks, and aircraft. By war's end, the groundwork was laid for an industrial cluster that today hosts roughly sixty refineries and chemical plants.

Across the border in the United States, the pressure to innovate produced technological leaps that would have lasting consequences. Catalytic cracking, alkylation, polymerization, and isomerization—terms that might have sounded like science fiction to the average citizen—allowed petroleum companies to turn heavy, ordinary oils into high-performance fuels. These fuels powered everything from jeeps to aircraft, lubricated artillery, and kept the machinery of war moving at a pace never before imagined.

The scale was staggering. During the conflict, the U.S. petroleum industry produced 60 percent of the world's crude oil and constructed the War Emergency Pipeline to circumvent shipping vulnerabilities. What began as a response to a global crisis became a laboratory for industrial expansion and technological experimentation. By the time peace returned, the Great Lakes region had transformed into a hub of petrochemical capacity and expertise, a legacy of innovation born from the pressures of necessity.

After World War II, the region entered a period of transformation that was as much social as it was industrial.[19] The petrochemical industry, which had already been shaped by wartime necessity, now became a magnet for workers seeking opportunity. In Sarnia, for instance, a village called Blue Water sprang up outside the gates of the first plant in Chemical Valley—a community built almost overnight to house the people fueling the industry's rapid expansion. It was a vivid example of how industry can literally shape the landscape of daily life, creating new towns, schools, and social networks almost as quickly as it built factories.

The postwar economic boom amplified these changes. Rising automobile ownership and suburban sprawl created an insatiable demand for petrochemical products—from plastics to synthetic materials—driving further investment in refining and manufacturing. By the late 1960s, the Great Lakes region had become one of North America's most significant petrochemical hubs. Cities like Chicago, Detroit, Toledo, Cleveland, Buffalo, and Sarnia were no longer just urban centers; they were nodes in a sprawling network of chemical production, connected by both geography and the flow of raw materials. In less than three decades, the region had transformed from a collection of industrial outposts into a continent-spanning powerhouse, a testament to the interplay between human ambition, technological innovation, and the relentless force of economic demand.

Sarnia might seem like any other industrial town at first glance, but step across the St. Clair River and you enter Chemical Valley—one of the most concentrated petrochemical hubs in North America. Its rise was hardly accidental. During World War II, the region had produced synthetic rubber for the Allied forces. After the war, that infrastructure became a springboard for an extraordinary expansion. By the early twenty-first century, Chemical Valley had packed its chemical and oil industries into a 15-mile corridor whose concentration of factories is almost dizzying in its scale.

The economic significance of this industrial cluster is correspondingly staggering. It produces roughly 40 percent of Canada's petrochemical output, a linchpin in the nation's industrial economy. But there is another, less celebrated side to the story. *Bridge Michigan* notes that "[the valley's] smokestacks cast a dystopian glow over Sarnia and across the St. Clair River to Port Huron" at night—a visual reminder of the environmental footprint of concentrated industry.[20] The very factors that made Chemical Valley a powerhouse—density, scale, and efficiency—also magnified its ecological and human costs. Nearby communities, including the Aamjiwnaang First Nation reservation, have felt these effects firsthand, highlighting the paradox at the heart of modern industrialization: Immense economic opportunity often comes paired with profound environmental and social responsibility.

At the turn of the twentieth century, the petroleum industry underwent a transformation that, in hindsight, seems almost ironic. Gasoline, once dismissed as a dangerous by-product with little commercial value, became the engine that would drive the industry—and, by extension, the modern world. The catalyst was the automobile. As car ownership exploded, so too did the demand for motor fuel. By 1911, gasoline sales had overtaken kerosene, and Standard Oil controlled 85 percent of Ohio's market, demonstrating how swiftly an overlooked waste product could become the cornerstone of a global industry.[21]

This was not just a change in products; it was a reorientation of the industry's entire focus. Refineries across the Great Lakes region expanded, pipelines were laid, terminals were built, and distribution networks grew increasingly sophisticated. What had begun as a local innovation in refining became a continental system, seamlessly moving crude oil from production centers to refineries, and then on to markets hungry for fuel.

The rise of gasoline reshaped more than the petroleum industry. It reshaped the region, the economy, and the very way people moved through space. And it all began with something that had once been considered little more than industrial flotsam, waiting to catch fire in the Cuyahoga River. The lesson, perhaps, is that value is often hidden in plain sight—and that transformation often comes from the least expected place.

For much of its early history, the Great Lakes petroleum industry was focused on refining oil that had been drilled elsewhere. Individually, by contrast, Michigan's industry began as a near afterthought—a state with minimal production, modest wells, and little national significance. And yet, over the course of the twentieth century, Michigan quietly transformed. According to the Clarke Historical Library, the state went from near obscurity to a major player, drilling over fifty thousand wells since 1925.[22]

The key to this transformation was buried deep beneath the surface—literally. Michigan sits atop a geological "bowl" of sedimentary rock, a natural formation that created ideal conditions for the accumulation of oil and gas. What had been an invisible feature of the landscape became the foundation for an integrated regional industry, linking domestic production with the refining and manufacturing hubs that had already taken root around the Great Lakes.

In 1976, the state introduced the Michigan Natural Resources Trust Fund, pioneering the concept of channeling oil and gas revenues into environmental protection and recreational resources. In one stroke, Michigan demonstrated that resource wealth didn't have to come at the expense of conservation. It was a lesson in balance, innovation, and foresight—and it highlighted a recurring pattern in industrial history: The most transformative developments often arise where natural advantage meets creative human policy.

By 2 a.m., on September 16, 1990, the *Jupiter* was secured.[23] Six mooring lines tethered the 392-foot tankship to the pier, a ritual of precision that signaled the next phase of its journey. The second mate met with a terminal representative, a quiet exchange of paperwork that transformed the abstract—barrels, cargo manifests, refinery logistics—into action. The unloading process began.

There was a rhythm to the work. A crew member clipped a bonding cable from the ship to the terminal, grounding it electrically, a small but crucial safeguard against disaster. Three others wrestled an eight-inch cargo hose into place, linking ship to shore. Then, with practiced hands, they opened the cargo tank and manifold valves. Gasoline began to flow.

Caution governed every movement. Gasoline, after all, is not just fuel but volatility in liquid form. At 3 a.m., that caution took on new urgency when a ship appeared on the horizon, moving steadily toward the *Jupiter*. The crew halted operations.[24] The cargo pump fell silent, waiting thirty-five minutes for the 638-foot *Irvin L. Clymer* to pass before work resumed.

By 4 a.m., the night shift gave way to fresh hands. Peter Walton, the first mate, relieved the second mate, while James Warren, a fifty-two-year-old pumpman, stayed on duty, his watchfulness uninterrupted. The hours stretched on. There were small interruptions at 5:10 a.m., with a power failure, and another at 6.[25]

Then came 8 a.m., a small reprieve from the relentless routine. Below deck, some of the crew gathered for breakfast—hot oatmeal, eggs, omelets, French toast, sausage, fruit, hashbrowns—a rare moment of comfort in a world dictated by schedules and machinery. But by 8:15 a.m., that moment was over. The cargo tanks were measured: twenty-two thousand barrels of gasoline remained.[26] The men returned to work. *Jupiter* had no time for lingering.

The Total Petroleum terminal sat on the west bank of the Saginaw River, a quiet but essential hub in Bangor Township's industrial landscape. Unlike the sprawling refineries that processed crude oil into finished products, this terminal functioned as a waypoint, receiving petroleum shipments primarily via pipeline. But for vessels like *Jupiter*, it was a familiar port of call.

At the heart of the operation was a 390-foot-long pier, rebuilt in 1986, designed with efficiency in mind.[27] Two pipelines extended from the dock—one for gasoline, the other for heating oil—ensuring a steady transfer of fuel from ship to shore. Its structure was practical, almost utilitarian: clusters of mooring piles to hold vessels in place, a series of safety mechanisms to keep operations running smoothly. By 1990, when the Coast Guard conducted its routine inspections, the verdict was clear: the terminal was complying. No discrepancies, no hazardous conditions, just the quiet hum of a system working as intended, a place where oil moved not with drama, but with precision.

Daniel A. Rentschler was new to the *Jupiter*, but he understood the job. Fresh from the Great Lakes Maritime Academy, he had stepped into his role as third mate with the quiet confidence of someone who had trained for this moment. On the morning of September 16, 1990, at precisely 8 a.m., he took over the watch from first mate Peter Walton. His shift complete, Walton was making his final preparations to leave the ship before its scheduled departure at noon.[28]

Rentschler's first order was straightforward but essential: The crew needed to check the fuel tanks, ensuring an accurate measure of the gasoline still in *Jupiter*'s hold. By 8:30 a.m., the task was done. Then—a sound. A distant whistle, cutting through the morning air. Instinctively, Rentschler looked up. A ship was approaching the Detroit and Mackinac railroad bridge.[29]

At that moment, three pumps on the *Jupiter* were running, steadily unloading its cargo. It was routine work, the kind of task that followed a well-rehearsed sequence—until something disrupted things. Rentschler, standing watch, saw the other ship closing in. Something about its approach wasn't right. He quickly issued orders: Thomas Sexton was to shut down one of the pumps and operate the forward winch. Randall J. Skinner was sent to stand by the aft mooring winch, ready for whatever came next.[30]

Then, Rentschler moved. He shut down the last two pumps and made his way to midship, where pumpman James Warren was stationed at the valve manifold platform. There, Rentschler started the hydraulic pump for the hose boom winch, a precautionary measure. Warren, watching the incoming ship, sensed the problem immediately. He raised his arms and began waving, a desperate attempt to signal the approaching vessel. Slow down. Pay attention. Something was about to happen.

It seemed as though the approaching ship was moving too fast. But speed on the water isn't just about velocity—it's about force, about the invisible chain reactions set in motion by a single miscalculation. As the vessel closed in, its wake rippled through the river. The water level surged upward by several feet, pressing against the *Jupiter* with unexpected power. The ship, momentarily unmoored by the sudden rise, rocked violently. First, it lurched backward—twelve feet, an unsettling drift. Then, just as quickly, it yanked forward, the momentum stretched its mooring cable to its absolute limit.[31]

The tension was too much. The center piling in the mooring cluster gave way, snapping under the strain. In an instant, the thick cable and the aft polypropylene line slipped free, vanishing into the churning water.[32] The *Jupiter*, now partially unmoored, was no longer entirely in control of its own fate.

Skinner had seen a lot in his years with Cleveland Tankers.[33] At sixty-one, he was a veteran of the job, someone who understood the subtle shifts of a ship under strain. But experience didn't make him any less alarmed when he saw the lines snap. Skinner rushed to activate the winches, hoping to regain some control. In the chaos, he caught sight of one of the mooring cables slackening, then heard the telltale splash as it disappeared into the water.

Up at the bow, Rentschler was watching it all unfold. He saw Sexton throw up his hands in frustration—a silent admission of helplessness. The message was clear: There was nothing more to be done. The *Jupiter* lurched forward again, but this time, something else gave way. One of the pier's pile clusters, unable to withstand the strain, buckled and tilted toward the vessel.[34] The polypropylene line, stretched to its breaking point, snapped free. But it didn't just fall—it recoiled violently, whipping through the air before crashing onto the ship's deck. Now, only a single line tethered the *Jupiter* to the pier.

Meanwhile, the *Buffalo* had already passed, its wake still rippling through the river. The *Jupiter*, caught in the current and no longer anchored at the stern, swung outward. Its aft section drifted further into the river, untethered, unrestrained. The ship was no longer where it was supposed to be.

Rentschler and Warren faced a simple mechanical dilemma—an overburdened hose boom. Their solution was straightforward: lower the boom to the deck, relieving some of the pressure. But the ship, still pressing forward, had other plans. The massive twelve-inch pipeline, tethered to the pier, strained against its foundation until it finally gave way, bending under the force and snapping a nitrogen purge line in the process.[35]

Gasoline began to spill—first in rivulets, then in sheets—spreading across the pier and the ship's deck, an invisible crisis unfolding in real time. But it wasn't just the hose line under pressure. The tension also pulled an electrical conduit free, an unnoticed detail in the chaos.[36] And then, in an instant, the unseen became undeniable: A single spark. A flicker of ignition. The gasoline erupted into flame, racing along the pipeline, consuming the ship's deck. What began as an effort to ease mechanical stress had, in mere moments, turned into a full-fledged disaster.

Rentschler was already moving—racing toward the bow of the *Jupiter*—when he glanced back and saw the ship's midsection consumed by fire. The sight was staggering. Flames licked at the steel, feeding on the fuel that had spilled just moments before. The ship had become a floating inferno.

He didn't hesitate. Gripping his handheld radio, he barked an urgent command to the terminal: shut the motor-operated valve. There was no time to wait for confirmation. He kept running, now joined by Sexton, the two of them pushing forward as the chaos unfolded behind them.

But in high-stakes moments, the difference between control and catastrophe can be razor-thin. Rentschler had a plan—to reach the ship's forward telephone, to call in the fire, to ready the bow anchor in case the ship drifted further. But before he could act, physics intervened.

A deafening explosion tore through the air. The force hit Rentschler like a tidal wave, lifting him off his feet and throwing him to the deck. In an instant, the situation had shifted again. The fire was no longer just a crisis, it was an unstoppable force, rewriting the course of events as it burned. Rentschler turned to Sexton, the fire raging behind them, and made the only call that seemed to make sense at the moment: get off the ship.

There was no time for life jackets, no time to grab a ring buoy. The flames had already rewritten the rules of survival. Without hesitation, the two men leaped from the burning ship into the frigid, dark waters of the Saginaw River. The current pulled at them, the cold shocking their systems, but they were free of the fire—at least for the moment. But survival isn't always about the choices we make. Sometimes, it's about the unpredictable forces that shape what happens next. Rentschler would live to tell the story. Sexton would not.

Experience teaches captains to trust their instincts, to read the subtle cues of a ship before trouble fully reveals itself. Captain David L. Beckwith, forty-four, had spent years with Cleveland Tankers, the last two and a half months commanding the *Jupiter*.[37] That morning, just before 8:30 a.m., his routine was unremarkable. He woke up, made his way to the galley, and casually instructed the cook to head ashore later for mail and groceries.

But then came the sound—low, strained, almost imperceptible to an untrained ear. A winch under pressure. Beckwith's mind processed it before he fully understood it. He rushed toward the aft passageway door and caught sight of the *Buffalo* passing by. Then, in an instant, the realization struck: *Jupiter was moving away from the pier.*

Beckwith sprinted to the pilothouse, intent on calling the *Buffalo*'s crew, but the moment he stepped inside, the situation escalated. The pier was breaking apart. The cargo hose, stretched to its limit, looked ready to snap. Instinct again took over—he grabbed the radio and called the Coast Guard. His vessel was no longer secure.[38]

Beckwith knew the next step: people. He ordered his crew to assemble at the stern for a head count. First mate Walton, who hadn't yet left the ship, and his replacement, George DeFrain, moved quickly, making sure every crew member had a life jacket or exposure suit.

Sometimes, history unfolds in the margins—witnessed not by those at the center of the action, but by people going about their daily lives, catching a glimpse of something before it becomes a catastrophe. Rose Cooper, a nurse, was doing something utterly ordinary that morning: approaching Independence Bridge in a car with her husband, waiting for a ship to pass.[39]

Cooper noticed the *Buffalo* first. It was moving, she recalled, "very, very slow." An observation so small, so seemingly insignificant, that it might have been forgotten—except for what happened next. She waited. The bridge remained open. And then, just as she was expecting the usual routine—the ship passing, the drawbridge lowering—everything changed.

The fire ignited. In an instant, the *Jupiter* was engulfed in flames. Without hesitation, Cooper reached for her camera. There was no time to think, no time to process what she was seeing. She snapped one photo, then another. Fourteen in total.

What she captured wasn't just an accident. It was a moment of transformation—the exact second when a slow-moving morning turned into disaster, when the *Jupiter* shifted from a working vessel to a burning wreck. And because she was there, in that in-between space, we have a record of what that moment looked like.

Disaster has a way of drawing people, sometimes out of duty, sometimes out of instinct. Dr. George Ascherl was navigating his forty-foot sailboat nearby when he saw it: the *Jupiter* on fire, a column of smoke rising into the sky. The first explosion had already torn through the ship, and now the crisis was fully unfolding.

He moved closer. Maybe he could help. Maybe there was still something to be done. Amid the chaos, he heard a voice from the burning ship calling out: *Stand by*.[40] But what struck him most wasn't the fire or the wreckage. It was a small, deliberate act of discipline and honor.

Before abandoning the *Jupiter*, the crew took a moment to lower the American flag.[41] Even as flames consumed the deck, even as survival instincts took over, they followed a ritual as old as seafaring itself. In that moment, Ascherl saw something beyond disaster—a quiet display of order in the face of chaos, a final gesture of control before the ship was lost.

Captain David Beckwith moved through the crew quarters, making sure no one had been left behind. The fire was raging now, the ship slipping further from salvation. There was only one thing left to do: *abandon ship.*

Among those who leaped into the water was Charles Prescott, the fifty-two-year-old chief engineering officer.[42] He had escaped through a hatch, only to find himself trapped in a ring of flames. The fire had surrounded him, turning the water into a deadly choice rather than a refuge. He jumped anyway. But survival is never guaranteed. As he plunged down, he struck his head against the ship's hull, vanishing beneath the surface.

At 8:50 a.m., Beckwith grabbed the radio and made his final call to the Coast Guard: *Men are in the water.*[43] It was a statement of fact. It was also a plea. Because now, the fate of his crew was no longer in his hands.

Onboard the *Buffalo*, Captain John MacFalda was focused on the routine task of navigating upriver. Behind him, third mate Richard Hollingsworth watched the ship's wake, scanning the water as he had done countless times before. And then, something caught his eye.

The *Jupiter*'s stern was moving—swinging out into the river in a way that ships aren't supposed to move. A fire flickered along the deck, small at first but spreading fast. Hollingsworth didn't hesitate. He turned to MacFalda and reported what he saw.

Seconds later, the situation escalated beyond words. The *Jupiter* was no longer just a ship in distress. It was engulfed—flames consuming it from end to end. And then came the explosion. In that instant, the haze of ordinariness surrounding the *Buffalo*'s journey was shattered. What had begun as another morning on the river had become something else entirely—a moment they would never forget, a disaster they could only watch unfold.

The bridgetender at Independence Bridge had heard countless whistles before. But when the *Buffalo*'s call echoed across the river that morning, something felt different. He picked up the phone and dialed 911.[44] Then he looked again.

The *Jupiter* was moving, drifting, untethered, its stern swinging out into the river. And then came the fire. Flames spread across the deck, turning a slow-motion emergency into a full-blown catastrophe. He called 911 again, this time with urgency: *The ship was on fire.*

But his job wasn't just to watch. He moved quickly, preparing the bridge for what was coming next. The fire crews. The rescue teams. The people who would try to contain what was already spiraling out of control. In that moment, he was no longer just an observer. He was the first link in a chain of responses, a quiet figure at the edge of disaster, making sure that when help arrived, the path was clear.

Some people step into a crisis not because they are asked to, but because instinct pulls them forward. Elmer Seltz, a terminal operator at Total Petroleum, had been close enough to see *Jupiter* drifting, breaking free from the pier.[45] He understood immediately what that meant. He ran.

Reaching the pier, Seltz focused on the mooring lines, scanning for any chance to regain control. But then his eyes caught something worse: the cargo hose, straining, pulling over the twelve-inch pipe. There was no time to think, only to act. He turned off the valves, shutting off the flow before the worst could happen.

But the worst came anyway. The fire ignited in an instant. Seltz grabbed his radio, his voice cutting through the chaos: *Fire! Fire*! Then, without hesitation, he moved again, isolating the pipe from the tank farm, severing a potential link in an even larger catastrophe. And still, he wasn't finished. As flames engulfed *Jupiter*, he ran toward the burning ship. Because in moments like these, some people don't run away. They ran toward.

On that frigid river, under a sky that had long since abandoned warmth, Rentschler and Sexton fought against forces greater than themselves. The water was relentless, their soaked clothing a cruel anchor pulling them downward. Rentschler, stronger in the water, pressed forward—but when he turned, he saw Sexton flailing, panic overtaking him.

Sexton was not a swimmer. He was a man out of his element, and in that moment, the river did what rivers do: It tested him. He cried out. Rentschler responded instinctively, grasping at his friend, but physics and desperation conspired against them. The weight of Sexton's body dragged them both under.

Then—Sexton vanished.[46] Rentschler, spent and shivering, clawed his way onto a piece of floating wreckage. He gasped for air, scanning the dark surface for his friend. But the river had already moved on.

Alan Garner was a man accustomed to managing crises. As the terminal manager, he was the one who made the calls and kept things running smoothly. But this was different. When he first heard reports of the fire, his response was procedural: dial 911. Yet from his office window, he could see that this was not a problem that could be handled from behind a desk.

Garner rushed to the pier, where he met Seltz. From there, they spotted Rentschler—a lone figure clinging to debris, the river deciding, for now, to keep him afloat. There was no hesitation. The two men climbed into a small boat, a Total Petroleum craft, and steered toward the drifting crewman. They pulled him aboard, his body spent, his breath shallow. But there was no time to dwell—there was still one man missing. They searched. They scanned the water, called his name, looked for any sign of movement. Nothing.

Instead, they turned to those they could save. Two more crew members, pulled from the cold, their survival hanging by moments. The cook helped to shore, his face a map of exhaustion and disbelief. And just like that, Sexton was gone.

Chapter 3

The Wrong Place at the Right Time

TODD SHORKEY'S SHIFT HAD BEEN QUIET—UNEVENTFUL, EVEN. A FULL TWENTY-FOUR hours on duty and now, as he sat at the kitchen table inside Wheeler Road's Fire Station 7 in Bangor Township, he was ready to wrap up. His coffee was warm, the station was coming to life with the next shift arriving, and in just a few minutes, he'd be heading out. Not home just yet, but close.

Then the alarm rang. A boat fire on the Saginaw River. "At first, we thought it was just a boat at one of the marinas—maybe a pleasure boat or something," Shorkey recalled years later.[1] But as they pulled out of the station, the morning calm shattered. A thick column of black smoke twisted into the sky. This wasn't just a boat fire. This was something else.

Firefighters from Essexville and Bay City were already being dispatched. The Bay City team felt an explosion before they even received the full details. "I remember feeling a bit nervous about it—fuel tankers, explosions, wondering what we were getting ourselves into," Shorkey admitted. It was that moment of hesitation, the split second where training collides with reality.

Bangor Township fire personnel didn't train for ship fires in those days. In the coming years, they would drill when possible for hypothetical incidents involving pleasure crafts as well as larger vessels. Ship fires, after all, aren't unheard of on the Great Lakes. The lakes have a long history of vessels meeting their end in fire and ice, and, in a twist of irony, the very first freighter recognized on these waters was lost in flames after running aground.

In November 1905, the steamer *R. J. Hackett* was making its way from Cleveland to Marinette, Wisconsin, loaded with coal, when disaster struck.[2]

A fire, born in the crew quarters, spread with terrifying speed to the oil in the engine room. The captain had no choice. He ran the vessel aground on Whaleback Reef, near Washington Island in Green Bay, a desperate attempt to salvage both ship and crew.

The thirteen men on board scrambled into lifeboats, the cold wind cutting through the night as a nearby fishing tug pulled them to safety. From a distance, personnel at the Plum Island Life-Saving and Light Stations saw the fire—flames licking at the sky, a floating inferno. They raced to the scene, but by the time they arrived, the stern was gone. Soon, the entire vessel had been reduced to nothing more than the charred remains at the waterline.

Today, what's left of the *Hackett* lies just off the reef, resting in ten to fourteen feet of water. Large sections of the hull, the steeple engine, the shaft, and the propeller remain—fragments of a story that ended in fire. Added to the National Register of Historic Places in 1992, the wreck is more than just a site for divers. It's a reminder of how quickly fire can turn a ship into history. But on this morning, Shorkey wasn't thinking about history. He was thinking about the fire ahead.

Fire at sea is one of the oldest and cruelest dangers in maritime history. And on the Great Lakes, it has played out again and again. On a summer day in 1919, the town of Port Colborne, Ontario, learned the terrifying power of something almost invisible: dust. The steamer *Quebec* was docked alongside a grain elevator, a concrete giant built to store over two million bushels of wheat, when the air itself ignited. What began as a few microscopic particles suspended in the stillness of the elevator became a chain reaction so violent that it sent flames hundreds of feet into the sky and scattered debris nearly two miles away.

Several people were killed instantly, many more left gravely injured, and the *Quebec*—a vessel built to withstand storms on the Great Lakes—was obliterated where it rested.[3] What happened in Port Colborne was more than an accident; it was part of a pattern, a chain of disasters born from a blind spot. The idea that dust—so ordinary, so unremarkable—could be as deadly as dynamite hadn't yet sunk in. By the time it did, the *Quebec* was gone, the grain elevator reduced to rubble, and the sky over Lake Erie filled with fire.

In the spring of 1947, the people of Texas City, Texas, gathered at the waterfront to watch a fire. It was mid-morning, a weekday, and from the dockside it looked almost theatrical: a French freighter, the SS *Grandcamp*, sat moored in the harbor with smoke rising from its hold. The smoke was strange—yellow and orange, curling like something out of a chemistry experiment—and so people stayed to watch. Firefighters climbed aboard. Longshoremen, following orders, had already walked off. The crowd thought they were at a safe distance.[4] They weren't.

At 9:12 a.m., the *Grandcamp* exploded. Not a puff, not a blast, but an event of such violence that it registered like an earthquake. The ship disintegrated. Nearly six thousand tons of steel were thrown into the sky—some of it at supersonic speed. A fifteen-foot wave slammed into the shoreline. Windows shattered in Galveston, eight miles away. Two airplanes flying overhead fell from the sky. And on the docks, from which the city's volunteer fire department had been fighting the flames, twenty-seven men vanished in an instant.

The *Grandcamp*'s cargo—2,300 tons of ammonium nitrate—was manufactured in Iowa and Nebraska, packed into paper sacks, and shipped south by rail. It was fertilizer, officially. But fertilizer has a double life. In the right conditions, it can nourish a field of corn. In the wrong conditions, it can level a city. Longshoremen in Texas City noticed the bags were warm to the touch. That should have been a clue. Instead, the sacks were stacked in the hold of a ship whose captain, worried about water damage, ordered steam—not water—to fight the fire when smoke first appeared. Steam does not extinguish ammonium nitrate. It feeds it.

What followed was a textbook case of how disasters cascade. The blast from the *Grandcamp* ignited oil tanks and chemical plants onshore. Hours later, another freighter, the *High Flyer*, packed with its own cargo of ammonium nitrate, caught fire and exploded as well—doubling the destruction. By the time the fires were out, nearly six hundred people were dead, hundreds more injured, and almost an entire city reduced to rubble.[5]

The *Grandcamp* was supposed to be part of a rebuilding effort, a ship reactivated after the war to carry supplies to Europe. Instead, it revealed something sobering about modern life: the hidden volatility of the everyday. Fertilizer. Twine. Tobacco. Cotton. The mundane cargo of global commerce turned into the fuel for one of the deadliest industrial accidents in American history.

On September 16, 1990, the first trucks from Bangor Township rolled onto the scene just minutes after the alarm sounded. Shorkey was in the second vehicle—a neon yellow rig known as Haz-Mat 7—its color a warning as much as an identifier. Close behind came crews from Essexville and Bay City, their sirens wailing against the morning air.

By 8:36 a.m., Alan Garner had already placed a critical call to the Bay County Sheriff's Office.[6] The first deputy arrived nine minutes later, took one look at the growing chaos, and immediately called for backup. Traffic on Bay City's bridges needed to be controlled, marine units needed to be mobilized, and the situation, still unfolding, demanded all hands on deck. The fire was no longer just a problem. It was an event. And in moments like these, the difference between control and catastrophe was measured in minutes.

Robert and Jean Colby were finishing their morning coffee when they heard the explosion. It was a sound that didn't belong—sharp, concussive, the kind that made you stop mid-sip and listen. From their boat at the Bay City Yacht Club, they turned toward the river and saw it: a thick plume of smoke rising upstream.[7]

For most people, that would have been the moment to step back. But the Colbys weren't most people. They had spent six years as Coast Guard auxiliarists, patrolling these waters, towing in stranded boaters, responding to distress calls. And then, over the radio, came the voice.

"Help us! Help us! We are on fire!" A pause. Then another transmission: "We've severed our mooring lines and are engulfed in flames. Get us help immediately!"

There was no hesitation. The Colbys moved as if on instinct, fired up their boat, and pointed it toward the chaos. Because when you spend enough time on the water, you understand one thing: When someone calls for help, you go.

The distress call crackled over the radio at the Saginaw River Coast Guard station, cutting through the routine of a quiet morning. The crew had been preparing their forty-one-foot patrol boat for a standard tour when the explosion ripped through the air. In an instant, their mission changed. By 8:51 a.m., the Coast Guard cutter and the Colbys' auxiliary boat had reached the *Jupiter*.

What they saw was chaos: sailors scrambling at the stern, waving their arms, before making the desperate decision to leap into the water. One by one, the rescuers pulled them aboard. In the frenzy, a panicked crewman, clawing his way to safety, yanked a watch clean off the wrist of one of his rescuers.

Among those aboard the cutter that day was Lynn Kulinec, a seventeen-year-old cadet from Millington High School.[8] She was still a teenager, but that morning, she would assist in the efforts to save the crew of the Jupiter, something that would later earn her the Honor Ribbon—the highest bravery award in the U.S. Naval Sea Cadet Corps at the time. As the cutter began pulling away, a last-minute movement caught the eye of those aboard the Coast Guard cutter. A man was waving, barely clinging to the burning wreckage. Without hesitation, the vessel pivoted, closing the distance to pluck him from the river before the flames could take him.

The cutter's fire monitor, a 2½-inch hose, was ready, but the decision was clear—fighting the blaze was secondary. The *Jupiter*'s crew was still in the water, and survival depended on speed. At 8:58 a.m., the Colbys' auxiliary vessel reported five people rescued, all in need of medical care.[9] The cutter had pulled in seven more, including a man with severe burns on his hands. Some were dazed, in shock, their bodies intact but their minds still trapped in the inferno they had escaped.

When the Coast Guard and auxiliary vessels finally reached shore, the next wave of responders was already in motion. Ambulance crews from Bay Medical Center stood waiting at the Wirt Stone dock, south of the Independence Bridge. As survivors were carried off the boats, the reality of the disaster set in. One ambulance wouldn't be enough. Calls went out for more. The *Jupiter* was still burning. But for those who had been pulled from the water, the worst was finally behind them.

At 9:12 a.m., Captain Beckwith made the call he had been trying to avoid.[10] Over the radio, his voice was steady but resolute: he was abandoning ship. The Coast Guard cutter, already positioned near the burning *Jupiter*, closed in, plucking Beckwith and five other crew members from the wreckage and ferrying them to shore.

On land, Beckwith wasted no time. He told emergency personnel that seventeen people had been aboard the *Jupiter* when the fire broke out. But then, after refusing medical treatment, he gave them the news they were desperate to hear: Everyone had made it off the vessel. At least, that's what he believed.

By 9:30 a.m., a second Coast Guard cutter arrived and made another discovery—three more crew members, waist-deep in the cold waters near the D&M railroad bridge. They were pulled aboard and taken to Station Saginaw River, shaken but unharmed. Still, something wasn't right. One name was missing from the roll call: Sexton. The Coast Guard launched a search, scanning the water, but there was no sign of him.[11]

Meanwhile, the *Jupiter* was growing more unstable by the minute. With fuel on board and the threat of another explosion looming, the Coast Guard issued a new directive: No vessel was to come within six hundred feet of the burning ship. From the shore, the crew watched helplessly as the tanker—once a formidable presence on the river—swayed dangerously in the smoke-filled air.

The fire was only part of the problem. As flames consumed the *Jupiter*, another threat loomed just beneath the surface—gasoline spilling into the Saginaw River. Bangor Township Fire Chief Jerry Ball understood the stakes. A fuel slick on the water could turn the river into a firestorm. He ordered oil containment booms to be deployed between the burning ship and the D&M railroad bridge, a move designed to stop the spill from spreading further downstream.[12]

But the river was wide, far wider than the firefighters initial estimates had accounted for. The first 1,500 feet of boom wasn't enough.[13] More was needed, and fast. Calls went out to outside agencies, and by 11 a.m., fire crews had doubled their initial effort—3,000 feet of boom stretched across the water, with four large barriers rigged in place to corral the gasoline.

Meanwhile, the firefighters on shore were facing their own grim reality. Bangor Township crews had positioned two five-inch fire monitors on the Total Petroleum pier, a last-ditch attempt to protect it from the searing heat radiating off the *Jupiter*. But even as they aimed their hoses, they knew the truth: They were outmatched.

"We sprayed water off the pier, but it wasn't really reaching the vessel," Todd Shorkey later admitted.[14] "It was more about trying to show we were doing something, but we didn't have the equipment to fight this fire. We were just trying to keep things safe as best as we could." In that moment, the men onshore weren't fighting to save the *Jupiter*. That battle had already been lost. Instead, they were fighting to make sure the disaster didn't get even worse.

The *Jupiter* was in peril. Drifting, ablaze, and barely tethered, it teetered on the edge of catastrophe. The nearly four-hundred-foot gasoline freighter, its metal hull glowing with heat, was held in place by a single cable at the Total Petroleum pier. A single cable.[15] The Coast Guard knew this was unsustainable. The winds—gusting between ten and eighteen miles per hour (mph)—pressed against the ship, urging it toward the river's current.

If the *Jupiter* broke free, it wouldn't simply be a runaway vessel; it would be a firestorm set loose on Bay City's most vulnerable points. Downstream sat the water treatment plant, a crucial piece of infrastructure that could be crippled by the burning wreck. Even more ominous was its proximity to the Rupp Oil Co. tank farm, where stored fuels lined the shore like dominoes, waiting for a spark.

The question was no longer whether action was needed. It was whether action would come in time. Chief Herb Mann and Petty Officer Paul Cormier knew the risks. So did Lieutenant Len Kilda and Captain Rick Hoppe. But knowing the risks and acting in spite of them are two different things.

The four men—two from the Coast Guard station in Essexville, two from the Bangor Township Fire Department—stood on the precipice of disaster. The *Jupiter*, still burning, still unpredictable, was an explosion waiting to happen. No one knew exactly how much gasoline remained onboard. A sudden detonation could turn the ship into a fragmentation bomb, sending fire, metal, and devastation in every direction. Yet securing the vessel was the only way to prevent an even larger catastrophe.

So they acted. Clad in fire- and heat-resistant suits, Mann, Cormier, Kilda, and Hoppe boarded a forty-one-foot Coast Guard vessel and edged toward the inferno.[16] The ship's hull radiated heat, the air thick with the acrid smell of burning fuel. Smoke billowed a hundred feet into the sky, a signal visible for miles. Timing was everything. They waited for the wind to shift, for the smoke and heat to be carried away from the ship's starboard side. Then, with deliberate precision, they moved in to secure the second cable—one step closer to saving Bay City from disaster.

Cormier had been six miles away when the *Jupiter* exploded. Off duty. On the opposite side of the river. But disasters don't wait for convenient timing. "I didn't know what I was getting into until I was there," he later said.[17] "I've always found myself in the wrong place at the right time."

What he got into was one of the most dangerous tasks of the night. The burning freighter needed to be secured, and Cormier was the one to do it. He sourced a three-hundred-foot wire cable from a nearby power company and a bulldozer from a local contractor. Then, armed with a .30-caliber harpoon-style gun, he fired the line toward the ship's anchor, hoping it would catch. It didn't. The fire had welded the anchor nearly in place.

A second attempt failed. The heat had turned the metal into something close to fused rock. If the cable couldn't latch on, there would be no way to pull the ship in. So Cormier did something audacious—with the cutter approaching the burning ship, he grabbed a crowbar, pried open just enough space in the melted steel, and fastened the hook. With the cable finally attached between the *Jupiter's* anchor and the bulldozer on shore, it was time to move the ship. "Once the tension was released, it was relaxed. I put in the half-inch line," Cormier recalled. "Then I ran that over to the Coast Guard boat, and they started pulling."

The men didn't have time to think about the risk. The flames roared beside them. The smoke thickened. The fire was still burning, but they had a job to finish. On shore, emergency crews cinched the line tight, and, using a pulley system, they pulled the *Jupiter* 135 feet closer to land. "I started out in a full asbestos suit," Cormier said. "That wasn't working. I took off the helmet, the gloves." It was heat. It was risk. It was raw survival. But the job wasn't over. The fire still raged.

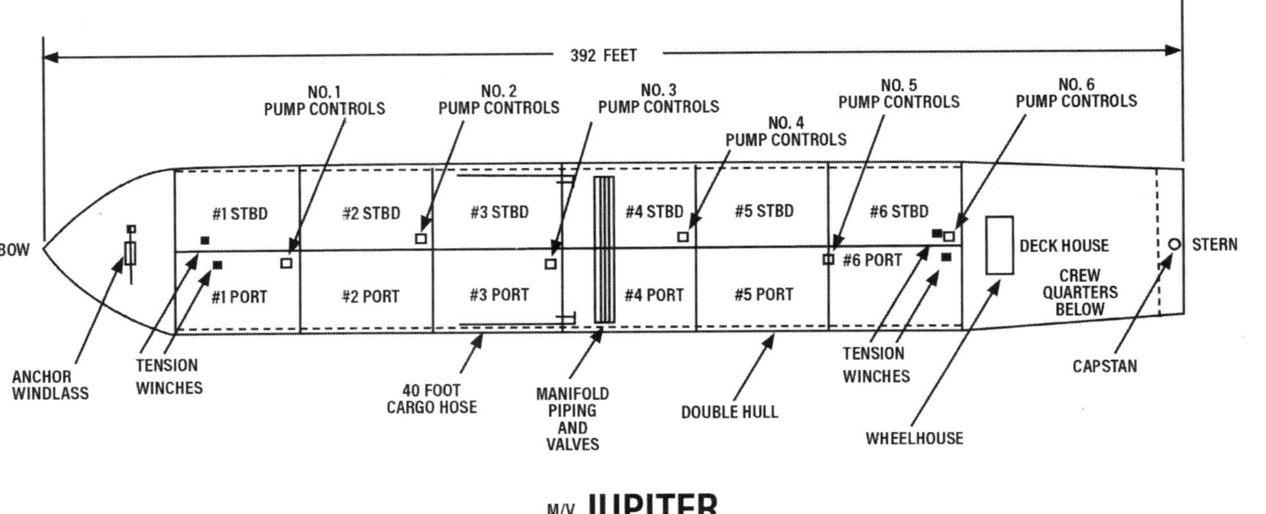

FIGURE 1. This diagram from the National Transportation Safety Board report shows the placement of pump controls, tension winches, and other equipment used by the crew of the *Jupiter* when it was unloading cargo on the Saginaw River. NTSB IMAGE.

BAY CITY
M.V. JUPITER

FIGURE 2. (*top, left*) Flames and smoke rose from the crippled tanker *Jupiter* on the Saginaw River in the hours after it exploded. U.S. COAST GUARD PHOTO.

FIGURE 3. (*bottom, left*) The charred remnants of one of the life boards aboard the *Jupiter* are pictured inside the Antique Toy and Firehouse Museum (Bay City, MI), where an exhibit is dedicated to the *Jupiter* disaster. AUTHOR PHOTO.

FIGURE 4. (*top, right*) The American flag removed from the burning tanker *Jupiter* by its crew before they abandoned the vessel now sits in the Antique Toy and Firehouse Museum. AUTHOR PHOTO.

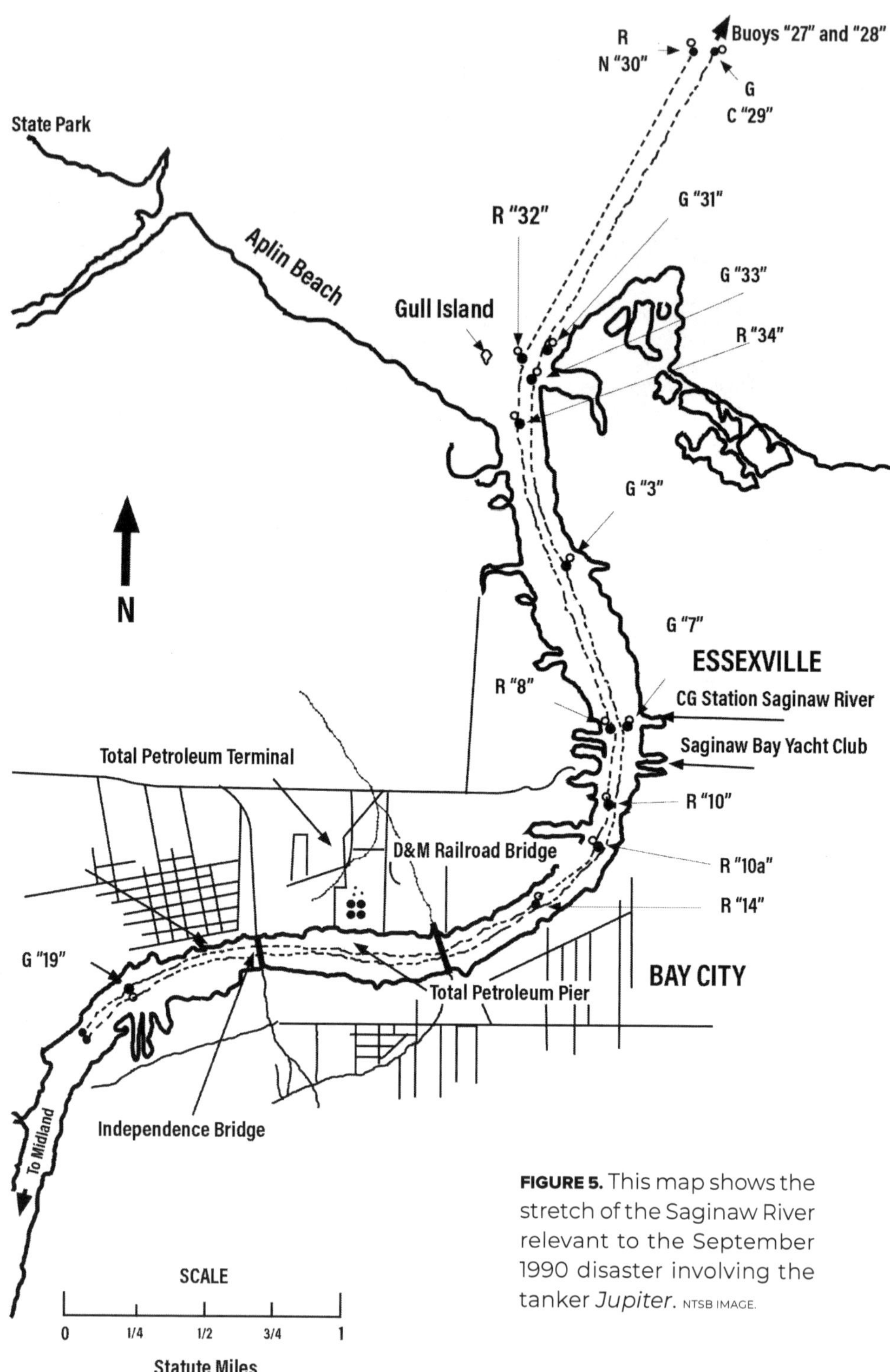

FIGURE 5. This map shows the stretch of the Saginaw River relevant to the September 1990 disaster involving the tanker *Jupiter*. NTSB IMAGE.

FIGURE 6. The pier once owned by Total Petroleum now sits unused on the Saginaw River. AUTHOR PHOTO.

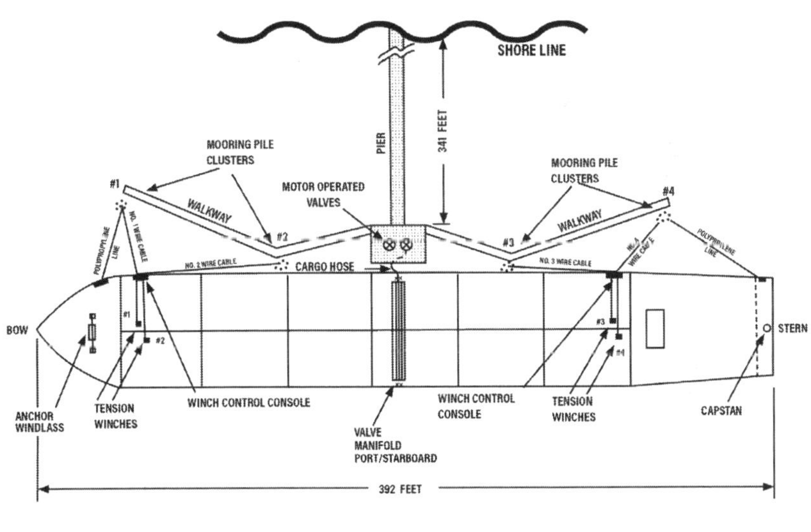

FIGURE 7. This diagram from the National Transportation Safety Board report shows the Total Petroleum pier and its association with the *Jupiter* on the morning of the disaster. NTSB IMAGE.

FIGURE 8. An aerial photograph shows the Jupiter ablaze after swinging into the middle of the Saginaw River on the morning of the disaster.

U.S. COAST GUARD PHOTO.

FIGURE 9. The *Jupiter* burns hours after exploding on the Saginaw River.

CHAPTER 4

Shadow Beneath the Surface

FIRES LIKE THE ONE ON THE *JUPITER* DON'T JUST GO OUT. THEY HAVE TO BE BEATEN into submission. And in this case, that battle required an army. So, firefighting experts from across the country—specialists from Texas, Coast Guard personnel, local emergency crews—converged on the Saginaw River, armed with thousands of gallons of fire-suppressing foam. The plan was simple in theory but grueling in execution: smother the flames before they could claim more ground.

By the time Williams, Boots, and Coots Inc.—a Texas-based commercial firefighting company—arrived just before midnight on September 17, the fire had already been raging for a full day. Their job was to prepare for a full-scale assault come morning. Meanwhile, the Coast Guard made ready its cutter *Bramble*, transforming it into a floating command center for the operation.[1]

At 8:15 a.m., crews loaded foam and essential gear onto the buoy tender. Just after noon, the *Bramble* set sail toward the *Jupiter*, pushing through the smoke-choked air. For nearly five hours, firefighters attacked the blaze, layering foam over the inferno, suffocating its oxygen supply. By 5 p.m., they made the call: The fire was out.[2]

But fire has a way of deceiving its enemies. Four hours later, at 9 p.m., the flames roared back to life. The *Jupiter* was not finished burning. And the battle was not over.[3] By the morning of September 18, the *Jupiter* had all but disappeared. The once-mighty vessel was now little more than a smoldering shadow beneath the surface of the Saginaw River, its hull believed to be resting on the riverbed.

At 1:30 p.m., the *Bramble* set out once again, returning to what remained of the burning ship. This time, the fight didn't last long. Within the hour, firefighters had finally conquered the flames. The Coast Guard's on-scene commander, alongside its Atlantic Strike Team, a group of specialized incident managers, remained vigilant, monitoring the wreck to ensure every last drop of gasoline was safely offloaded.

But the fire was only part of the story. Ashland Petroleum Company had another request: find the missing crew member. The Coast Guard wanted to search, but they faced an impossible obstacle. The personnel on site were exhausted, drained from two days of relentless firefighting. Worse, they lacked the proper diving gear and training for such a recovery mission. The fire was out, but its aftermath had only just begun.

The next day, as crews worked to clean the gasoline that had leaked into the Saginaw River, they found him. Thomas Sexton—forty-six years old, a seasoned seaman, a husband, a father—had died swimming toward shore after the explosion. His body was recovered sixty yards north of the *Jupiter*'s wreckage. That same day, two of Sexton's crewmates, James Warren and Charles Prescott, were discharged from Bay Medical Center with minor injuries. A third, Ahmed Mohammed, remained under hospital care. But the wounds left by the *Jupiter*'s explosion were not only physical.

Originally from Hawthorne, California, Sexton had moved to Bonaparte, Iowa, in 1946. After high school, he spent four years in the U.S. Coast Guard before setting out to sea. He earned a history degree in 1978 from the University of Northern Iowa, taught as a substitute teacher, and spent nineteen years as a relief seaman for Ashland Oil. He loved books. He loved history. He was a man of knowledge and travel, always moving between past and present, land and water. He left behind a wife, Paula, and a ten-year-old son, Timothy. A father. Two sisters. A life cut short, a name added to the ledger of those lost at sea.

For Charles Prescott, survival carried its own burden. The burns healed, the bruises faded—but the explosion stayed with him. The images played on a loop in his mind. He sought help, saw a therapist, and was diagnosed with acute post-traumatic stress disorder. The lake called to him, but the memory of the *Jupiter* wouldn't let him go. For a year, he stayed away. Then, finally, he went back.

Every industrial boom leaves behind a shadow. For the Saginaw River and Bay, that shadow took the form of toxic sediments, algae blooms, and collapsing fisheries. By the mid-1980s, the accumulated weight of a century's worth of industrial discharge, agricultural runoff, and habitat destruction had become impossible to ignore. In 1987, under the Great Lakes Water Quality Agreement, the Saginaw system was officially designated an Area of Concern (AOC)—a label reserved for only the most environmentally compromised waterways in the region.[4]

The criteria were stark: fish that couldn't be eaten safely, beaches that couldn't be used, wildlife populations that were visibly declining. Fourteen potential "Beneficial Use Impairments" had been identified across the Great Lakes, and Saginaw checked off twelve of them.[5] It was less a checklist than a diagnosis—a reminder of how thoroughly economic growth had been achieved at the expense of ecological health.

And yet, the designation was not merely an indictment. It was also an invitation. By naming Saginaw one of the system's most damaged rivers, policymakers established a framework for repair and recovery. Progress has been uneven: as of 2025, only three of those use impairments have been lifted. But the effort reflects a larger truth about the Great Lakes—that the same forces capable of reshaping entire landscapes through industry can, if redirected, be marshaled toward restoration.

When we think about pollution, we often imagine a single, catastrophic event: a smokestack explosion, an oil spill, a dramatic moment of rupture. But the Saginaw River and Bay show how contamination creeps in slowly, almost invisibly, until the accumulation becomes impossible to ignore. The list of pollutants reads like a chemist's inventory: dioxins, furans, polychlorinated biphenyls (PCBs), heavy metals, acids, and nutrients like nitrogen and phosphorus. They arrived from everywhere at once—factories, municipal outfalls, farm fields, even storm drains. Each on its own might not have been enough to push the river to crisis. But together, over decades, they layered into a toxic sediment at the bottom of the watershed.

One of the most infamous culprits was Dow Chemical.[6] For decades, the company's operations in Midland sent dioxins into the Tittabawassee River, which in turn carried them downstream into the Saginaw. These compounds, among the most toxic chemicals ever created, don't dissolve or degrade; they sit in the sediment, leaching upward, a kind of chemical inheritance passed from one generation of river life to the next.

Then there were the PCBs from General Motors plants. Designed to make machines run more smoothly, PCBs instead found their way into fish and birds, accumulating in fat tissue, moving up the food chain. Three GM facilities along the river became notorious contributors, leaving behind a legacy of industrial by-products that could never be entirely contained.

And if industrial waste wasn't enough, the land itself inadvertently conspired. Fertilizers from surrounding farms washed into the watershed, feeding algae blooms that robbed the river of oxygen. In 2012, water testing revealed something almost too blunt to require interpretation: fecal material, both bovine and human. "Poop," one local outlet put it plainly. People were swimming in it.[7]

What makes the Saginaw River's contamination remarkable isn't just the sheer number of pollutants, but the way they converged—industrial by-products, agricultural runoff, municipal waste, all flowing into the same body of water and creating a chemical cocktail that was both invisible and undeniable. It's a reminder that environmental crises are rarely the work of one bad actor; more often, they're the sum of a thousand ordinary decisions, layered together over time.

Think about a bald eagle for a moment. A bird that sits at the very top of the food chain, majestic, untouchable. Yet in the Saginaw Bay watershed, that same eagle is vulnerable—not because of predators, but because of dinner. Every fish it eats carries a trace of poison, and with each meal those toxins accumulate, magnifying up the chain until the hunter itself becomes the victim.

This is the paradox of the Saginaw River and Bay. The contamination that seeps invisibly into the water doesn't just stay there. It travels—into the muscles of fish, into the eggs of birds, into the very structure of the ecosystem. The consequences have been stark enough that health authorities long ago issued sweeping warnings: don't eat the fish. Not some species, not sometimes—all of them, across the river and many in the bay. What was once a source of food became a vector of disease.

For wildlife, the problem is even more insidious. Pollutants disrupt reproductive cycles, weakening the very capacity of species to persist. Bald eagles, the emblem of resilience, find their eggs thinning, their hatchlings fewer. The chemistry of contamination plays out not in laboratory beakers but in nests and spawning beds.

And then there is the landscape itself, which has shifted in ways that make recovery harder still. Coastal marshes have been drained or degraded. Exotic invasive species—goby, ruff, zebra mussel—have rewritten the food chain. And the rocky reefs that once offered safe nurseries for native fish now lie smothered under layers of sediment, the biological equivalent of a blanket pulled too tightly over a newborn's crib.

The story of the Saginaw is not just one of toxins, but of accumulation—chemicals in bodies, silt on reefs, invaders in marshes—each layer compounding the last. What emerges is an ecosystem caught in a feedback loop of decline, where the greatest threat to survival comes not from the dramatic but from the quiet, persistent weight of contamination itself.

Sometimes the biggest changes to an ecosystem don't come from factories or smokestacks, but from something as small as a fingernail-sized mollusk. In the late 1980s, zebra mussels slipped quietly into the Great Lakes, stowed away in the ballast water of transoceanic ships.[8] No one paid much attention at first. But within a few years, they were everywhere—clinging to pipes, coating boats, smothering native mussels. They were, in a sense, the perfect infiltrators: tiny, prolific, and devastatingly efficient.

Zebra mussels are voracious filter feeders. They clear water of plankton so effectively that the surface seems almost cleaner, more transparent. But what looks like clarity is really emptiness. The plankton they consume are the foundation of the aquatic food chain, the invisible engine that drives everything from minnow to walleye to the bald eagle. By stripping it away, zebra mussels rewrite the rules of the river.

And they are not alone. Round gobies and ruffs—two other uninvited guests—have entrenched themselves in the Saginaw watershed as well, competing with native fish, stealing spawning grounds, reshaping predator-prey dynamics. Layered on top of chemical contamination and the slow erosion of habitats, these invaders turn the river into something unrecognizable, a system that bears little resemblance to the Saginaw Bay of a century ago.

Another contamination on the lakes and rivers of the Great Lakes region? Something much more artificial. To fight the *Jupiter* fire, firefighters turned to one of the most effective tools in their arsenal: 3M Light Water foam. It looked like shaving cream, but its purpose was far more serious. Designed for high-intensity industrial fires, the foam was sourced from fire departments and factories across multiple states and rushed to the scene.

The response was led by Boots and Coots, a company with deep expertise in battling oil and gas fires. Their crews sprayed the foam deep into the ship's burning remains, while specialists moved in to inspect the damage. The science behind it was simple but powerful—97 percent water, 3 percent organic compounds, forming a thin film that cuts off the fire's oxygen supply. The foam was considered mostly biodegradable, engineered to vanish along with the flames it subdued.[9] But what no one was talking about in 1990—what few even knew—was what else was in that foam.

Every great industrial breakthrough starts with a discovery so useful it seems almost magical. For PFAS—per- and polyfluoroalkyl substances—that moment came in the 1940s.[10] Chemists stumbled upon compounds bound together by carbon and fluorine, a pairing so stable that nature itself could barely undo it. The carbon-fluorine bond is one of the strongest in organic chemistry, a kind of molecular superglue. To engineers, that strength was a gift. To the environment, it would turn out to be a curse.

In the decades that followed, PFAS became the industrial world's Swiss Army knife. They repelled water and oil. They withstood heat and chemical attack. They worked as surfactants, slipping easily into manufacturing processes where other chemicals failed. A single class of compounds could make a raincoat truly waterproof, a frying pan genuinely nonstick, a piece of military equipment nearly indestructible. The possibilities were so varied that production spread with remarkable speed.

But persistence—the very quality that made PFAS so useful—was also what made them dangerous. These were not chemicals that washed away or broke down. Once created, they stayed. They lingered in soil and water, and eventually in human blood. Internal company research confirmed this as early as the 1970s. At 3M, scientists dosing rats and monkeys with PFAS reached a sobering conclusion: The compounds "should be regarded as toxic."[11] Yet outside the company walls, the discovery remained unspoken.

The nickname would come later: "forever chemicals." It captured both the marvel and the menace of PFAS. What began as a triumph of ingenuity had, almost imperceptibly, laid the groundwork for one of the most enduring environmental challenges of the modern era. By the middle of the twentieth century, PFAS had made a quiet leap—from the laboratories of chemical giants into the living rooms and kitchens of ordinary Americans.

Between the 1960s and 1990s, these compounds became so ubiquitous that they defined, in many ways, the texture of modern life. They hid in the surface of your frying pan, in the fibers of your carpet, in the box that held your

Friday-night pizza. They made your raincoat bead water effortlessly, your sofa resist stains, your popcorn bag hold grease without collapsing. At some point, almost without noticing, every household in America became a showcase for PFAS.

The Great Lakes region sat at the center of this transformation. Michigan and Wisconsin's paper mills churned out grease-resistant packaging for hamburgers and french fries. Textile factories treated fabrics with PFAS to make them waterproof and wrinkle-free. In industrial towns around the lakes, chrome-plating shops relied on PFAS to keep their processes clean and efficient. And perhaps most consequential of all, airports, refineries, and military bases sprayed thousands of gallons of firefighting foam infused with PFAS—an invisible insurance policy against catastrophe and an enduring one, since the foam's chemical legacy lingered long after the fires were gone.

It's easy to miss the moment when a breakthrough ceases to be extraordinary and becomes ordinary. PFAS had crossed that threshold by the late twentieth century. What began as a remarkable laboratory innovation had, by the 1990s, become the chemical equivalent of wallpaper: everywhere, indispensable, and almost entirely unnoticed.

In 1973, the U.S. Air Force published a report that, in hindsight, reads like the opening chapter of a doomsday novel. The report was straightforward: Aqueous film-forming foam—AFFF, the firefighting miracle infused with PFAS—was toxic to fish.[12] The solution, the authors suggested, was simple enough. Use carbon filters in drinking water systems, and contamination could be prevented.

Over the next five years, more reports followed. The U.S. Navy, too, tested the foam. The results were the same.[13] Fish died. Toxicity confirmed. The warnings were written down, filed, and shelved. And then . . . nothing changed. The foam kept flowing, at air bases and naval yards, in hangars and training facilities. Firefighters doused flames with it. Pilots trusted it to save their lives. It was, after all, too useful to abandon.

The disaster of PFAS in the Great Lakes had been quietly unfolding for decades, hiding in plain. Yet it took until 1998 for 3M to alert the Environmental Protection Agency (EPA) that PFOS—the company's flagship chemical—was showing up in the blood of ordinary Americans.[14] The announcement was carefully measured: The levels were "very low," the studies of company workers showed "no adverse effects," and the company insisted there was no substantial risk to health or the environment.[15]

But inside the company, scientists had long known that these chemicals persisted, accumulating silently, like a debt no one wanted to pay. And then came 1999. Richard Purdy, a 3M environmental specialist, quit in frustration. His letter read less like a resignation and more like a warning. Officials, he wrote, were "unethical," prioritizing markets and public image over environmental safety. PFOS, he argued, were "the most insidious pollutant since PCB"—polychlorinated biphenyl, the notorious chemical that had already wreaked havoc in the Great Lakes.[16]

But in 1990, in Bay City, no one was immediately concerned about the ramifications of using the foam to extinguish flames on the burning ship. In fact, there were more pressing concerns about other matters—less hazardous, but much more visible. The fire sent thick, black smoke billowing into the sky, and when the rain came, it brought something else with it: an oily, sooty residue that coated everything in its path.

The American Automobile Association (AAA) of Michigan and State Farm Insurance in Bay City were flooded with calls. South End residents reported strange black stains on their cars and homes. A painting crew from C&M Home Services, in the middle of a $2,000 job, had to start over—washing and repriming an entire house after the residue ruined its fresh coat of paint.[17]

Local cleaning companies were overwhelmed with inquiries. A car dealership in the South End had no choice but to wash every vehicle on its lot. Even in Saginaw Township, miles away, people noticed it. One woman stepped outside and found the mysterious grime on her patio furniture.[18] The explosion had sent fire into the sky. Now, its remnants were falling back to earth.

The *Jupiter* fire wasn't just a local event—it was a spectacle. Its smoke, thick and unrelenting, could be seen from fifty miles away. And yet, for all its scale, health officials insisted the impact on Bay City residents was minimal. The air, they said, remained safe. The smoke, despite its ominous reach, carried no immediate threat.[19]

Hospitals and clinics saw only a handful of cases—people with asthma, emphysema, or other preexisting conditions who found the air a little harder to breathe. Bay City allergist Richard Horbal treated a couple of patients for coughing and wheezing. Around ten more showed up at Bay Physicians Medical

Center in Essexville with similar complaints. Doctors expected symptoms to clear up within a week. No lasting effects. No crisis.[20]

The real danger, experts believed, was to those closest to the flames. Rescue personnel, firefighters, and emergency crews bore the brunt of exposure. One worker was treated for smoke inhalation at Bay Medical Center and released. Dr. Vaughn Wagner, from the state Department of Public Health, noted that gasoline fires like this one produced far more particulates than, say, a car fire. But the wind had done its job, carrying the worst of the smoke away before it could settle over the city.[21]

Still, there were precautions. Cleanup crews wore respirators. They provided urine samples to monitor potential exposure. The state Department of Natural Resources (DNR) began testing for benzene, a petroleum-based chemical, though they expected to find little more than carbon and water among the fire's remnants.

In the end, Bay City had been lucky. The fire was massive, the smoke unavoidable, but the wind had played its role as an unexpected ally—blowing the problem somewhere else. But one group had no chance to escape the blast. No time to react. No warning. The fish.

When the *Jupiter* exploded, the shock wave ripped through the water with devastating force, killing more than forty thousand fish within a hundred-yard radius of the vessel.[22] The explosion wasn't just fire and smoke—it was pressure, a violent underwater concussion that left its victims with no visible burns, no trace of gasoline poisoning, just catastrophic internal damage.

A report from the DNR would later confirm the gruesome details. The fish suffered severe hemorrhaging—bleeding in their eyes, gills, muscles, even their brains.[23] Terry L. Walkington, district supervisor for the Surface Water Quality Division, authored the report in December, but it wasn't made public until after a law enforcement review.

James P. Baker, an acting district fisheries biologist, led a Fish Mortality Investigation on September 20. His findings were striking: There were no signs of fuel exposure. The fish didn't smell of gasoline. There were no abnormalities in their organs. The only cause of death was the blast itself.[24]

When the Animal Diagnostic Laboratory in Lansing reviewed the evidence, its conclusion was the same. No toxins. No lingering pollutants. Just trauma.[25] For Bay City residents, the *Jupiter* disaster was a story of fire and survival. But for thousands of fish in the Saginaw River, it was over in an instant.

On the evening of September 19, a gasoline spill—originating from the wreckage of the *Jupiter*—seeped into storm sewers, setting off a chain reaction of containment efforts, environmental concern, and government response.[26] It was, in many ways, a classic case of how small variables—wind direction, infrastructure, and human decision-making—can conspire to create an event much larger than itself.

By the following day, cleanup crews had already managed to remove most of the contamination. They had vacuumed fifteen thousand gallons of a dark, sludgy mix of gasoline, water, and soot from the Saginaw River. The true volume of gasoline that had entered the storm sewers, however, remained a mystery. Booms had been deployed to keep the spill contained, but nature had its own plans. Strong winds stirred the water, pushing gasoline-tainted runoff back into the drains, forcing officials to act fast.

The contamination, while minor, carried an invisible but potentially dangerous risk—fumes. To counteract this, emergency crews flushed the storm system with firefighting foam, a tactic designed not just to clean, but to suppress any chance of explosive vapor buildup. Officials quickly reassured the public that there was no immediate threat, but the spill had already set into motion something bigger: a conversation about preparedness, response, and the unforeseen challenges of managing an environmental crisis.

On the morning of September 20, something strange appeared in the water near the wreckage of the *Jupiter*. A dark, swirling substance—thick and unplaceable—floated just beyond the tanker. Was it ash? Gasoline? Some unpredictable chemical cocktail of both? No one was quite sure.[27] But the mere sight of it was enough to spark concern. If it drifted too far, it could reach Saginaw Bay, and then the situation would change entirely.

At first, containment seemed to be holding. Five booms had been deployed to trap any pollutants, and initial reports suggested that the barriers had done their job. But uncertainty lingered. Aerial photographs hinted that small amounts of the substance had slipped past, their dark trails barely visible against the water's surface.

Then came the debate. Bay City Fire Chief Jerome Marchlewicz, along with representatives from Ashland Oil, stood firm: This was ash, nothing more. A by-product of the tanker's fiery end, harmless in the grand scheme of things. But a state water analyst wasn't so sure. From his perspective, there was reason to believe the substance contained gasoline and other fluids, hidden within the residue.

And so, the situation shifted from containment to uncertainty, from cleanup to a question of trust. In the days following the explosion of the *Jupiter*, the question soon became, Was the worst truly over? Ashland Oil representatives were quick to reassure the public. The fire, they argued, had likely consumed most of the vessel's fuel. There were no cracks, no leaks, nothing left to fear.

But then, on September 21, reality told a different story. Small cracks *were* found in the wreckage, and through them, gasoline began to seep into the water.[28] It wasn't a catastrophic breach, but it was enough to reignite concerns. Emergency crews worked quickly to contain the black, oil-streaked substance drifting into the Saginaw River. Ashland teams repositioned containment booms, tightening their defenses against the spill. Early tests suggested that gasoline levels outside the booms remained low, but that was little comfort. Cleanup crews pressed on, vacuuming the contaminated water, knowing that the real test was yet to come.

By October, reinforcements arrived. A team of Florida-based salvors was brought in with a massive task: pumping at least three million gallons of gasoline-tainted water from the wreck into Bay City's wastewater treatment plant.[29] But before any of that could happen, there was another battle to fight—one not in the water, but in the boardroom. City commissioners demanded guarantees. Would Bay City be on the hook for environmental damage? Who would pay if something went wrong? After negotiations, Cleveland Tankers, the *Jupiter*'s owner, agreed to cover any environmental or equipment-related costs. Only then did the real work begin.

In the end, the numbers told a complicated story. Of the *Jupiter*'s original one million gallons of unleaded fuel, the explosion had incinerated most, leaving just fifty thousand gallons behind.[30] Some of that fuel inevitably found its way into the river, but officials remained confident: The impact would be minimal. Gasoline, after all, is lighter than water. It evaporates. It disperses. It doesn't sink and linger the way crude oil does. Between containment booms, aggressive vacuuming, and constant monitoring, the damage was, by all accounts, controlled.

And yet, as experts reviewed the test results, a larger truth emerged—one that defines environmental disasters of this kind. The *Jupiter* explosion had been serious, but it could have been much, much worse. The difference between catastrophe and near-miss is often razor-thin, shaped by a mix of physics, luck, and the speed of human response. Bay City had walked that line. And this time, at least, it had come out on the right side.

Much of the focus was on the gasoline spill, the cleanup efforts, and the environmental impact. But for the surrounding community, there was another crisis unfolding—one that had nothing to do with fuel or contamination and everything to do with timing. The wreckage of the *Jupiter* lay squarely in the Saginaw River, a vital artery for the region's shipping industry. And with the waterway closed, the effects rippled outward.

This wasn't just an inconvenience—it was a logistical nightmare, hitting at the worst possible moment. The shipping season was still in full swing. Marine terminals and commercial docks, many of which handled asphalt, concrete, and stone, were now cut off from their supply lines at the peak of construction season.[31]

For marinas catering to pleasure boaters, the impact was milder. The season was already winding down, and poor weather had kept many late-season boaters off the water. But for businesses dependent on cargo shipments, the disruption was immediate and costly. Bay Aggregate, for instance, had been supplying limestone for a major repaving project on U.S.-10.[32] With its usual dock inaccessible, the company was forced to lease space downstream—an expensive and inefficient work-around that highlighted just how critical the river was to local industry.

The closure stretched from five hundred yards upstream of the Independence Bridge to five hundred yards downstream of the D&M railroad bridge, effectively shutting down a key stretch of the waterway.[33] Days turned into weeks. The *Jupiter*'s wreckage wasn't removed until October 17, and even then, the river remained closed until the U.S. Army Corps of Engineers could ensure it was clear of debris. It took another five days before the U.S. Coast Guard finally gave the all-clear on October 22, marking the end of a thirty-seven-day shutdown.[34]

By then, the damage had already been done. Supply chains had been rerouted, construction projects had been delayed, and businesses had been forced to adapt to a crisis they never saw coming. The wreck of the *Jupiter* may have been an environmental emergency, but in many ways, it was also an economic one—a reminder of how fragile infrastructure can be, and how a single unexpected event can send shock waves through an entire system.

The *Jupiter* was never going to be a simple cleanup job. By the time Titan Maritime Industries arrived in Bay City, the wreck had already become more than just a burned-out husk in the Saginaw River—it was a logistical puzzle, a chemical hazard, and, at times, an unpredictable force of nature. The biggest problem? Gasoline.

Even after the explosion, an estimated forty-five thousand to fifty thousand gallons of unleaded fuel remained on board. Before any salvage work could begin, that fuel had to be removed. But gasoline isn't just a liquid—it's a vapor, an ever-present risk hanging in the air, waiting for the smallest spark. So before the operation could even begin, Titan crews coated the ship with fire-smothering foam, a layer of protection against the invisible threat of combustion. Nearby, a team from Boots and Coots—the legendary oil well firefighters—stood by, just in case something went wrong.

The process was painstaking. Crews pumped gasoline from the ship's compartments into waiting trucks. But the *Jupiter* itself was unstable, its structure weakened by fire and time. If too much weight was removed too quickly, the ship could break apart or even slip loose from its resting place. To counterbalance the loss of gasoline, Titan's crew pumped water into the ship's six compartments as they worked, keeping the vessel in equilibrium. By nightfall on October 1, they had removed between sixteen thousand and seventeen thousand gallons. It took days to finish the job, air-blasting the compartments to eliminate the last traces of gasoline vapor.[35]

And then, just as one problem was solved, another emerged. The *Jupiter* still held twenty-three thousand gallons of diesel fuel in its engine room, along with lubricating oils that had to be extracted.[36] Only once the ship was fully emptied could it be moved to the scrap yard at H. Hirschfield Sons Co., where its undamaged metals would be salvaged—some repurposed for repairs on other ships, some melted down and sent into entirely new industries.

Yet, as with everything involving the *Jupiter*, nothing went smoothly. Rainstorms raised the river's water levels, forcing Titan's crew to build a sandbag dike along the deck to keep water from flooding the wreck.[37] Then an unusual current—between four and six knots, far stronger than what was normal for this stretch of the Saginaw—swept through, tearing apart the pipeline that was pumping gasoline-tainted water from the wreck to the Bay City's wastewater treatment plant. Operations ground to a halt until the current slowed.[38]

Finally, on October 17, two tugboats from Detroit—the *Carolyn Hoey* and *Susan Hoey*—pushed the *Jupiter* to the north side of the river.[39] Its bow and stern were secured to pilings at Total Petroleum and Rupp Oil, tethered to a barge to ensure it stayed in place. Only then could Titan begin the final phase: scanning the riverbed with sonar for debris large enough to threaten passing vessels. A crane was brought in to remove whatever remained below the surface.

And yet, the *Jupiter* still had one last act. On July 9, 1991—months after the wreck had been removed from the river and sat ashore in Bay City, readying to be scrapped—oil in the ship's bilge caught fire.[40] The Coast Guard and local firefighters responded, but by the time they arrived, the flames had already begun to die out. No one knew exactly what had sparked it. In a way, it didn't matter. The fire didn't cause any real damage. It didn't delay the cleanup. But it did reinforce what everyone involved in the *Jupiter* salvage already knew: This was a ship that refused to go quietly.

Disasters don't just leave behind wreckage and environmental concerns—they leave bills. And the *Jupiter* was no exception. The cost of battling the fire and managing its aftermath climbed to at least $6.1 million, a staggering sum that underscored just how complex and resource-intensive the response had been.[41]

At the center of it all was Ashland Oil Co., the parent company of Cleveland Tankers Inc., which owned the *Jupiter*. The company had little choice but to reimburse public agencies for the extraordinary expenses incurred during the crisis. Overtime pay for police and fire departments alone accounted for much of the $940,000 that flowed back to local, county, and state agencies. But the invoices submitted to Ashland told a more detailed story—$105 for telephone calls, $285 for two tow trucks, more than $1,000 for floodlights, barricades, and sandbags.[42] Every item, no matter how small, represented a piece of the larger machine that had been set in motion to contain the disaster.

Then there was the ship itself. The *Jupiter* had been valued at $5 million.[43] Some of that loss may have been offset by the sale of scrap metal from the wreckage, but if anyone knew the exact numbers, they weren't saying. What was clear was that the ship, once an asset, had become a financial liability overnight.

The U.S. Coast Guard's response alone carried a price tag of $786,000, with a majority—$675,000—going toward equipment expenses.[44] The agency had deployed the cutters *Bramble* and *Bristol Bay*, which played a crucial role in fire suppression efforts. Helicopters were dispatched from Detroit and Traverse City, while a massive C-130 cargo plane flew in from Clearwater, Florida, ferrying personnel and supplies. Their mission extended beyond firefighting—they provided aerial surveillance, ensuring that responders had a full view of the unfolding situation.

And the costs kept piling up. Travel expenses reached $44,000. Personnel costs hit $56,000. Coast Guard officials remained stationed in Bay City for thirty-seven days—September 16 to October 19—until the *Jupiter* was finally removed from the shipping channel.[45]

Even as the immediate crisis faded, the operation continued. Small boats patrolled the river around the clock, enforcing the designated safety zone—a thousand-foot stretch between the Independence Bridge and the Detroit and Mackinac railroad bridge. The river had to be watched. Other vessels had to be kept away. The job wasn't over just because the flames had been extinguished.

This is the hidden cost of a disaster like the *Jupiter*. The fire itself lasted hours. The response took weeks. The expenses stretched on for months. And in the end, what remained wasn't just the charred skeleton of a ship, but a long, itemized record of everything it took to clean up the mess.

Disasters rarely unfold in isolation. There is always a before, a chain of events that lead up to the moment when everything goes wrong. In the case of the *Jupiter*, that moment came on the night of September 16, when an explosion turned the tanker into a fireball on the Saginaw River. But in the days and weeks that followed, a new question emerged: Who was to blame?

From the very beginning, officials from American Steamship Co., owners of the *Buffalo*, were clear on one thing—their ship wasn't responsible.[46] In formal hearings, they pushed back hard against the idea that the *Buffalo*'s speed had anything to do with the explosion. Instead, they pointed the finger at the *Jupiter*'s crew, alleging improper mooring procedures had set the stage for disaster.

Ashland Oil, the parent company of the *Jupiter*'s owner, saw it differently. The day after the explosion, an Ashland vice president argued that the *Buffalo* was moving fast enough to generate a wake strong enough to pull the *Jupiter* away from its mooring at the Total Petroleum terminal.[47] If true, it was a serious accusation—one that placed responsibility for the explosion not on the tanker's crew, but on the freighter passing by.

American Steamship officials fired back. The *Buffalo*, they insisted, had been traveling at "dead slow"—a cautious 1 to 2 mph, the minimum needed to maintain control in the river's current and avoid drifting into the Independence Bridge.[48] Company records, they added, showed no history of speeding violations by the *Buffalo*'s operators. Any complaints about wakes only became official if they involved injuries or financial damages.

Yet, the river had its own version of events. That summer, several boaters on the Saginaw had lodged complaints about the *Buffalo*, claiming its wake had damaged their vessels.[49] Whether that was relevant to the *Jupiter* explosion, however, remained an open question. "But whether that's what happened in this case hasn't been confirmed," one official admitted.

At the time, the section of the river where the explosion occurred had no official speed limit. But it did have a no-wake zone. A ship moving at three to four knots could generate a wake strong enough to cause problems. And in a moment where everything lined up just wrong—where a tanker was moored in just the wrong way, where a freighter passed at just the wrong speed, where the physics of water and momentum combined in just the wrong proportions—that wake might have been all it took to turn a routine night on the river into a catastrophe.

On September 18, Captain John MacFalda sat before investigators from the U.S. Coast Guard and the National Transportation Safety Board (NTSB), answering the question that had loomed over the investigation since the moment the *Jupiter* burst into flames: Had the *Buffalo* caused the disaster? MacFalda's answer was simple. "I don't believe the passage of my vessel had any effect on that day," he stated.[50]

The hearings had begun just two days after the explosion, as federal agencies worked to untangle the events that had turned an ordinary night on the Saginaw River into catastrophe. MacFalda's testimony was key. As the captain of the *Buffalo*, he could either confirm or dismantle the theory that the freighter's wake had played a role in destabilizing the *Jupiter*.

His version of events went like this: That morning, as the *Buffalo* entered the Saginaw River, he made his way to the pilothouse. The ship continued to slow as it approached a railroad bridge, moving at what he estimated to be just 2 to 3 mph—hardly fast enough, he argued, to generate a wake that could dislodge a tanker.[51] When the *Buffalo* passed the *Jupiter*, it did so at a distance of sixty to sixty-five feet.

Then, something unusual happened. The *Buffalo* had traveled about a ship's length beyond the tanker when the *Buffalo*'s third mate noticed something: The *Jupiter* was drifting away from the dock. And then—moments later—the explosion.[52]

Despite the chaos, the *Buffalo* kept moving. It continued upstream to the Midland Contracting pier, where it unloaded its thirteen-thousand-ton cargo of coal. That decision, more than anything else, drew scrutiny. One attorney later described it as a "hit and run"—a sharp accusation that suggested the *Buffalo* had caused the accident and then simply moved on.[53]

But was that what had happened? Or was the *Jupiter* already a disaster waiting to happen, set into motion by forces that had nothing to do with the *Buffalo* at all? The hearings sought to answer that question. But in the end, as with so many disasters, the truth would not be simple. By the second day of hearings, a new theory had emerged—one that shifted the focus away from the *Buffalo*'s wake and toward something far more fundamental: the condition of the dock itself.[54]

The mooring posts at the Total Petroleum Co. terminal were supposed to hold a vessel as massive as the *Jupiter* securely in place. Instead, evidence suggested they may have been little more than rotting wood, waiting to give way at the wrong moment. Lawyers representing maritime unions didn't hold back, calling the terminal "defective" and arguing that Total Petroleum bore some responsibility for what had happened that night.[55]

Witness after witness described unsafe conditions at the dock. Richard Hollingsworth, third mate of the *Buffalo*, put it bluntly: Great Lakes seamen considered the terminal a navigational hazard.[56] He had been in the pilothouse when the freighter passed the *Jupiter*, and he knew the risks of docking at that pier.

Then came the most telling detail. A state DNR investigator reported that when the *Jupiter* pulled away from the dock, a cluster of wooden mooring posts came with it. Sergeant Lawrence Terlecki, who inspected the scene after the explosion, described what he found: dry-rotted oak posts, weakened by time and exposure, incapable of holding the tanker in place.[57] One post had been sheared in half, a clear sign that the *Jupiter*'s mooring had failed—not because of the *Buffalo*, but because the infrastructure itself had crumbled.

And then there was Daniel Meyers, the *Buffalo*'s wheelman. Before the explosion, he had noticed something small but unsettling—a slack mooring line connecting the *Jupiter* to the dock.[58] In that moment, it was just an observation, a quiet note of concern. In hindsight, it may have been the first visible clue of a disaster waiting to unfold.

On September 20, Dr. George Ascherl Jr., a neuroradiologist from Bay City, took the stand. He was not a sailor by trade, but on the night of the *Jupiter* explosion, he had been on the water, close enough to witness the moment disaster struck. Ascherl had set out that evening from the Saginaw Bay Yacht Club aboard his vessel, the *Wild Irish*.

Timing, as it happened, had placed him directly behind the *Buffalo*. He saw the freighter pass, observed its crew, and noted something critical—there was no visible wake.[59] This was an important detail. Much of the investigation centered on whether the *Buffalo*'s wake had destabilized the *Jupiter*, causing it to drift from the dock. But as the *Wild Irish* followed in the *Buffalo*'s path, Ascherl saw nothing to support that theory.

Then, as his boat neared the *Jupiter*, it happened. The tanker caught fire. Within moments, flames raced across the deck and onto the pier. As alarms blared, crew members scrambled toward the stern—the only remaining refuge as the inferno consumed the ship. And then, the first explosion. A massive, deafening blast, followed by several smaller eruptions, each one sending more fire into the night sky.

Even at a distance of three hundred to four hundred feet, Ascherl and his passengers felt the heat, an oppressive, searing force radiating across the water. In an instant, the routine passage of ships along the Saginaw River had turned into something else entirely—a catastrophe unfolding in real time, with no clear explanation and no way to stop it.

Elmer Seltz, the operator overseeing the Total Petroleum terminal at the time of the *Jupiter* explosion, stood at the center of a complex narrative involving caution, uncertainty, and a tragic chain of events. On September 21, during his testimony, he recounted the moment the ship caught fire—a moment that, like so many in the business of oil transfer, was defined by a series of precarious decisions.

Seltz recalled hearing a ship's whistle while in the pumphouse and turning just in time to spot the *Buffalo* moving swiftly under a railroad bridge downstream. "I said to myself, 'My God, I'm sure he's going too fast,'" he reflected—a fleeting, intuitive judgment, as he later recalled, that captured the tension of the moment. The scene that followed played out with almost cinematic clarity.[60]

Seltz made his way to the pier, where he witnessed the *Jupiter*—the massive tanker that would soon be at the heart of the disaster—suddenly lurch backward, then pitch forward violently. This unsettling motion was accompanied by a distinct, mechanical sound: The pipe securing the cargo hose began to bend, and gasoline, under pressure, sprayed uncontrollably from the hose. In an instant, the situation escalated from routine transfer to catastrophe. A flash, and then, an explosion of fire.

His reaction was immediate. "Fire!" he shouted into his two-way radio, reaching for the control valves that governed the flow of fuel into the terminal's tanks. His task now was simple in concept, but complicated in execution: to prevent further disaster. In these moments, the responsibility for regulating the transfer of gasoline fell to the *Jupiter*'s crew. They had the tools to stop the flow—either by shutting off the ship's fuel pump or pressing a button to close a motor-driven valve on the dock. But this was where the ambiguity crept in. Seltz could not definitively confirm whether the pumps were on at the time of the explosion. He acknowledged the uncertainty, adding a crucial detail: When docking, tankers are typically advised to shut down their fuel pumps as a safety precaution, particularly when another vessel is passing.[61]

In that uncertainty lies the heart of the issue. The question of whether the pumps were running at the moment of the explosion, and whether the crew of the *Jupiter* followed protocol, would never be fully answered. What remained were the consequences of those few moments of indecision and the terrible chain of events they set in motion—a story not only of human error but of a system where the smallest details can tilt the balance between safety and disaster.

David Beckwith, captain of the *Jupiter*, offered his testimony on September 25, a moment that would provide a crucial piece of the puzzle in the events leading up to the catastrophic explosion of the tanker. He described something extraordinary—something that, in his decades of experience, he had never encountered before: the *Buffalo*'s speed on the Saginaw River. "I had never seen a vessel move as fast as the *Buffalo* did," Beckwith remarked, emphasizing the unnerving force of the passing ship.[62]

This wasn't just a passing ship, however. The *Buffalo*'s wake—its forceful suction—had an unexpected consequence. Beckwith testified that as the *Buffalo* thundered by, the dock at the Total Petroleum terminal, where the *Jupiter* was unloading its precious and volatile cargo of gasoline, was literally torn apart by the power of the passing ship. The scene had all the hallmarks of a disaster in slow motion—one that no one could have predicted with certainty, but one that was nonetheless set in motion by a complex interplay of forces.

Standard procedure in such situations was straightforward: When another vessel passes, the gasoline discharge pumps on the tanker should be shut off. It's a rule, a safeguard designed to prevent precisely the kind of disaster that later unfolded. But in a moment that would haunt Beckwith, he had to admit that he could not say for sure whether the *Jupiter*'s pumps had been turned off when the *Buffalo* passed.[63] In that admission lay a telling truth: In moments of chaos, even the most established procedures can slip from memory, and even the most practiced crews can find themselves unsure of the details that separate safety from calamity.

What Beckwith's testimony revealed was a larger pattern: how small lapses—imperceptible in the heat of the moment—can become the flashpoints of larger, more catastrophic outcomes. The combination of a speeding ship, a dock vulnerable to sudden forces, and an unclear adherence to protocol became the cocktail that ultimately led to the explosion. And in that mix, Beckwith's uncertainty about the pumps is a reminder of the fragility of even the most rigid systems when confronted by the unpredictable forces of human behavior and nature.

Al Garner, the supervisor on duty at the Total Petroleum dock, testified that when another vessel had passed earlier, the *Jupiter* radioed to confirm it would shut off its pumps. However, Garner said no such call was made when the *Buffalo* passed.[64] The hearings into the explosion of the *Jupiter* then drew to a close on September 27 with a chilling testimony from James Warren, the pumpman who had been at the center of the disaster.

Warren, who suffered burns to his hands, face, and hair, offered a firsthand account of the chaotic sequence of events—one that would forever alter his life. His testimony began with the arrival of the *Buffalo*, a coal freighter that approached the Total Petroleum terminal with alarming speed.[65] As the ship neared, Warren, in a moment of instinctive caution, signaled for it to slow down. But his warning was ignored. With the *Buffalo* barreling ahead, Warren and his colleague, Thomas Sexton, acted quickly to shut off the gasoline pumps, following protocol as best as they could under the circumstances.

Then came the moment that no one could have predicted. As the *Buffalo* passed and the *Jupiter* was pulled away from the dock, the pipeline on the terminal's dock cracked under the strain. It was a small detail, seemingly insignificant—until it wasn't. Within moments, fire erupted on the dock, and in a terrifying flash, it "jumped to the ship."[66] The flames leaped from the dock to the *Jupiter*, and then, as though propelled by some unseen hand, the tanker's cargo hose burst, sending gasoline into the air in a dramatic, violent arc.

It was chaos. As flames rapidly spread across the ship's deck, Warren shouted for his crewmates to activate the firefighting foam system. In the next instant, he found himself engulfed by the flames. "I got caught in it. I was on fire some, and I put myself out," he recalled, his voice steady but the memory of the searing heat unmistakable.[67]

In the midst of the inferno, Warren's instincts kicked in. He grabbed a life jacket, but hesitation crept in. Would jumping into the water cause more harm than good? Fear of injury held him in place, but only for a moment. Realizing there was no other option, he slid down a mooring line into the river below. It was a desperate move, but it was also his escape. A Coast Guard boat soon arrived, pulling him from the water and transporting him to the hospital, where he would receive treatment for his burns.

Warren's testimony was not just an account of personal survival. It was a reflection of the chaotic and unpredictable nature of the disaster. In the end, it underscored a central truth: In high-stakes environments like this, it is often the smallest missteps, the most fleeting moments of uncertainty, that set the stage for catastrophic outcomes. Warren's actions that day were a testament to his quick thinking and resolve, but they also painted a stark picture of how swiftly disaster can unfold when human error, environmental factors, and mechanical failures collide.

In the aftermath of the *Jupiter* explosion, those waiting for answers were forced to endure months of uncertainty. The investigation that followed was a slow, methodical process—one that seemed to stretch time itself. Investigators from the U.S. Coast Guard in Chicago and the NTSB in Washington, D.C., delved into a mountain of reports, sifting through details and searching for clarity. They had originally expected to release their findings by March 1991, but as with so many high-stakes inquiries, their timeline slipped. The reason? A hydrodynamic study, essential to understanding the role the river's currents played in the disaster, was incomplete.[68] This study was designed to analyze how the water moved when the *Buffalo*—that fateful coal freighter—passed by the *Jupiter* moments before the explosion.

What seemed like a straightforward scientific inquiry turned out to be a pivotal piece of the puzzle. How did the river's currents affect the *Jupiter*'s mooring? What role did the mooring play in the chain of events that led to the disaster? These were the questions the study sought to answer, but they weren't easy to address. So, the investigation stretched into another month, pushing the expected release date into April.

Then, after months of anticipation, the report finally arrived in October 1991—an almost anticlimactic end to a drawn-out process.[69] By the time it was released, much of the world had already moved on. But for those who had lived through the *Jupiter* explosion—the survivors, the families, the investigators—those months of waiting were more than just a test of patience. They were a reminder of how, in complex investigations like this one, the search for truth is rarely linear. It's a process of uncertainty, of waiting for the right pieces to fall into place, and of learning that sometimes the most critical answers lie in the smallest of details—the way water moves, the ripple effects of a ship's wake, the unseen forces that shape the course of history.

CHAPTER 5

The Investigation

OVER A YEAR AFTER THE *JUPITER* EXPLOSION, THE NATIONAL TRANSPORTATION SAFETY Board (NTSB) finally released its highly anticipated marine accident report—ninety-two pages of meticulous analysis titled "Explosion and Fire Aboard the U.S. Tankship Jupiter." It was a document that seemed to have taken on a life of its own in the months leading up to its release. The investigation, while thorough, was also a reflection of the challenges inherent in uncovering the full complexity of such a catastrophic event.

The NTSB, an independent federal agency tasked with improving safety across all modes of transportation, was not a new player in the realm of accident investigation. Since its founding in 1967 and its subsequent mandate under the Independent Safety Board Act of 1974, the NTSB had become a crucial institution for uncovering the causes of transportation accidents, issuing safety recommendations, and assessing the effectiveness of government agencies in safeguarding the public. Its process was methodical and comprehensive, focused on a singular goal: understanding what went wrong and how to prevent it from happening again.

The *Jupiter* report, when it finally emerged, did more than recount the fire and explosion. It delved into a series of interconnected safety issues that had contributed to the disaster. The report examined the suitability of the berthing facilities at the Total Petroleum terminal in Bay City: Was the dock fit for purpose? Were the mooring procedures for the *Jupiter* and the Total Petroleum pier adequate?

The speed and trajectory of the *Buffalo*, the freighter whose passing had triggered the sequence of events, came under scrutiny. But perhaps most telling of all was the absence of a communication system to alert a vessel moored at a bulk fuel terminal when another ship was approaching in the channel. This gap in communication was a key point that underscored how even small failures in operational systems could lead to catastrophic consequences. In addition to these concerns, the report raised alarms about local disaster contingency plans and the lack of flame screens in the ullage pipes aboard the *Jupiter*—a safety measure that could have mitigated the explosion.

The NTSB's response to these findings was clear and direct. It issued a series of safety recommendations to a wide range of stakeholders: the U.S. Coast Guard, Total Petroleum, Cleveland Tankers, the Lake Carriers' Association, the State of Michigan, and Bay County Emergency Services. These recommendations were not merely suggestions; they were calls to action, designed to address the systemic flaws that had been laid bare by the explosion.

In many ways, the release of the report marked the beginning of a new chapter—a process of reform, change, and vigilance. But it also served as a reminder of the complexity of safety and the multitude of factors that must align perfectly to prevent disaster. The *Jupiter* explosion wasn't just a failure of one ship or one company; it was a failure of systems, communication, and oversight—an intricate web of vulnerabilities that, when left unchecked, can lead to tragedy.

The investigation into the *Jupiter* explosion was not simply a matter of collecting testimony or examining the obvious physical damage; it involved a meticulous analysis of materials and forces, each piece of the puzzle shedding light on a different aspect of the tragedy. One particularly telling investigation component focused on the broken center mooring pile at Total Petroleum's tanker berth—a seemingly inconspicuous piece of the infrastructure that turned out to be more significant than anyone had initially realized.

To better understand what had gone wrong, investigators sent a sample of the broken wood from the No. 4 pile cluster to the U.S. Department of Agriculture's (USDA's) Forest Products Laboratory in Madison, Wisconsin.[1] The USDA's role in the investigation was less about the immediate fire and explosion, and more about understanding the integrity of the infrastructure that had failed. The lab's analysis identified the wood species and confirmed what many had suspected: the presence of decay.

The USDA lab report went even further, revealing that "the characteristics of the wood cells at the fracture zone suggest the wood was affected by brashness"—a term used to describe a brittleness brought on by decay.[2] Yet, despite its careful examination, the USDA lab was unable to pinpoint exactly how much strength had been lost due to the wood's deterioration, leaving an unresolved question about the extent to which decay had played a role in the structural failure.

Meanwhile, Total Petroleum was not taking any chances. In an attempt to understand the precise physical dynamics that led to the explosion, the company enlisted a naval architect from the Massachusetts Institute of Technology (MIT).[3] This wasn't just any architect, but someone equipped with the kind of advanced technical expertise needed to probe the deep hydrodynamic interactions between the *Buffalo* and the *Jupiter*. Using a cutting-edge computer simulation, the naval architect recreated the events of that fateful moment when the *Buffalo* passed the *Jupiter*, calculating the forces at play in the waterway.

The results of this hydrodynamic study were not merely academic; they were part of a larger effort to grasp how such complex, almost invisible forces had contributed to the chain of events that led to the disaster. Together, these tests—on materials, forces, and simulations—painted a picture of an intricate, interwoven series of failures: a weakening mooring pile, the undetected impact of decay, and the unseen forces at work in the water. These weren't just mechanical failures—they were a reflection of how vulnerability, hidden in plain sight, can combine with a seemingly routine series of events to cause catastrophic outcomes.

The investigation into the *Jupiter* explosion was marked by a fascinating contrast in methodologies—each approach designed to illuminate the complex interactions at play during the fateful moments leading up to the disaster. While Total Petroleum enlisted a naval architect from MIT to study the hydrodynamic forces between the *Buffalo* and the *Jupiter*, the American Steamship Company (ASC), which owned the *Buffalo*, sought a separate analysis.[4] In this case, the ACS turned to a consultant from Ann Arbor, Michigan, who used a different computer program to model the interaction between the two vessels.

The ASC's consultant focused on the key moments when the two vessels interacted: first, when the *Buffalo* approached the *Jupiter*; second, when it passed alongside the *Jupiter*; and third, when the *Buffalo* finally cleared the *Jupiter*. These were the critical instances where hydrodynamic forces—the invisible pressure fields created by the movement of ships through the water—could escalate and cause significant damage.

Hydrodynamics, the study of how water interacts with objects moving through it, plays a crucial role in the safe transfer of liquid bulk cargoes like gasoline. The forces generated when a large vessel passes a smaller one can cause a ship to surge or sway, which, without proper controls, could lead to disaster. The *Jupiter*'s mooring system was designed to mitigate this movement, but it relied heavily on steel wire cables, spring lines, and winches to control the vessel's motion. These systems were meant to absorb the force of the ship's movement along the pier, preventing excessive surging and minimizing the risk of damage or spillage. But as the report would reveal, the *Jupiter*'s mooring system, though designed with care, was underprepared for the force of the *Buffalo*'s passage.

The consultant's study showed that as the *Buffalo* approached, it generated an upstream surge force that caused the *Jupiter* to move slightly forward—an effect partially resisted by the No. 2 and No. 4 mooring cables.[5] But as the *Buffalo* passed, the hydrodynamic forces reversed, pulling the *Jupiter* backward with great force. The No. 3 cable, tasked with resisting the aft movement, was under extreme stress. Yet, the winch controlling the No. 3 cable had been improperly released, allowing the cable to slacken and giving way to the *Jupiter*'s backward motion. By the time the *Buffalo* created a maximum upstream surge force, the *Jupiter* was caught in an uncontrollable swing, moving forward once more—only to encounter a dangerous yawing motion as the forces pushed the *Jupiter*'s bow toward the shore and its stern into the river.

It was a perfect storm of engineering failures and unforeseen forces. When the *Jupiter*'s stern swung wildly out into the river, the mooring systems designed to hold it steady couldn't absorb the shock. The No. 4 mooring pile—already compromised—finally gave way. The No. 4 steel cable and the polypropylene line that had been attached to it fell into the water, leaving the *Jupiter* vulnerable to the forces that now controlled its movement.

In retrospect, it became clear that the design of the mooring system was flawed. The Total Petroleum berth, which had only four pile clusters, was insufficient to secure the vessel properly.[6] The positioning of the piles meant that the bow and stern lines were anchored to the same points, creating a lack of redundancy and leaving the vessel exposed if one of the mooring lines failed. The system was also underpowered for a tanker of the *Jupiter*'s size, and the failure of a single mooring point could—and did—have catastrophic consequences.

In many ways, the *Jupiter* explosion was a tale of compounded vulnerability: the limitations of the berth design, the failure of key mooring lines, and the unforeseen consequences of hydrodynamic forces. When these elements combined, the ship's security was fatally compromised, leading to a chain of events that no one could have predicted—but that in hindsight were perhaps more inevitable than anyone would have imagined.

It became clear that the mooring system at the Total Petroleum terminal had not kept pace with the size of modern vessels. The terminal had long been accustomed to handling smaller ships, but as larger vessels like the *Jupiter* began to dock, the mooring setup should have evolved to ensure their safety. The NTSB's report suggested a simple yet critical upgrade: adding an extra pile cluster at each end of the berth, extending beyond the *Jupiter*'s bow and stern. This would have allowed for more secure positioning of the polypropylene lines and provided additional mooring points—an essential step for ensuring that the *Jupiter* could be properly aligned and secured both fore and aft.

At the heart of the issue was the configuration of the lines that were meant to control the *Jupiter*'s movement. The forward polypropylene line, angled slightly backward, and the No. 1 wire cable, angled slightly forward, were intended to act as breast lines.[7] In theory, these lines would prevent the ship from drifting backward and keep it close to the pier. In practice, they fell short. The angles of these lines were insufficient to control the ship's aft movement. Had the forward polypropylene line been secured ahead of the *Jupiter*'s bow, it might have provided the necessary resistance to minimize the backward motion, especially when the *Buffalo* passed. But this was an oversight—one that would have grave consequences.

Over the years, the Total Petroleum terminal had seen countless ships dock without incident. The Coast Guard had visually inspected the pier and mooring equipment, but there was a critical blind spot: the wooden mooring piles.[8] These piles, a staple of the terminal's infrastructure, were never subjected to thorough internal inspections. Eventually, the wear and tear of time and weather began to take its toll. The USDA laboratory's tests on the broken pile revealed signs of rot, though the lab couldn't pinpoint the exact degree of decay. What was clear, however, was that the deterioration had compromised the integrity of the mooring system, leading to the pile's eventual failure.

This was a crucial moment in the investigation: It wasn't just the visible wear on the pile that mattered, but the hidden decay within it. The report called for more rigorous testing of wooden piles, recommending that marine construction companies regularly inspect their pier and mooring equipment for internal decay. Moreover, it urged the Coast Guard to incorporate evaluations of mooring devices into routine terminal inspections to ensure their effectiveness and prevent further failures.

The breakdown in the mooring system didn't happen in isolation. The testimony from the crew that day painted a vivid picture of the chaos on board.[9] One sailor, assigned to operate the aft winch controls, described how, when the winch motors were engaged, the winch brakes released automatically. This allowed the wire cables to unspool from the winch drum, increasing the slack in the No. 3 mooring cable. The tension on the cable was key to keeping the *Jupiter* in place, but as the cable loosened, it couldn't resist the vessel's motion.

It was here that the timing of events became critical. One sailor testified that he had no time to react before the No. 4 mooring pile failed. Yet, the fact that he had started the winch motor suggested that, in his panic, he may have moved the control lever into the payout (unspool) position. This would have relieved tension on the line just as the vessel surged aft, allowing the cable to pay out rapidly. The resulting slack in the No. 3 cable created a splash, a sound that was heard by the third mate. This sound, combined with the crew's actions, suggested that the No. 3 cable was rapidly unspooling, even as the vessel's motion reversed.

At the winch controls, one crewman stood between the *Jupiter*'s two critical mooring wires. As the tension on the No. 3 cable dissipated, he found himself directly in the line of fire if the wire snapped back. The fact that he was in such close proximity to the taut wire added an additional layer of danger to an already volatile situation.

In moments of crisis, it is easy to forget that much of what happens on a ship is governed not by the human hand alone, but by a complex interplay of mechanics, intuition, and instinct. The sailor manning the winch controls on the *Jupiter* that day was no novice—he understood, with the clarity of experience, that if the No. 3 wire cable detached from the mooring pile, it would recoil violently toward him. A sudden snap, and the taut steel line could strike with the force of a whip. Yet, when the ship surged backward and the winch began to pay out the wire, he did what seemed most prudent: He released the cable to reduce strain, hoping to prevent it from breaking under the pressure.

But this act of caution—this attempt to manage the ship's movement by loosening the wire—was, in hindsight, the tipping point. The safety board, in reviewing the events, surmised that the sailor had unwound the cable not to slow the ship, but to relieve the tension, an action that allowed the wire to slacken as the *Jupiter* surged.[10] The result was predictable: The wire fell into the water, creating the splash that alerted the third mate to something amiss.

The third mate, upon hearing the splash, immediately suspected a malfunction, but it was quickly ruled out. The No. 3 winch had functioned perfectly when securing the ship before the *Buffalo*'s approach, so the problem lay elsewhere. The splash, then, could only have been the result of the sailor's intervention with the winch. His decision to release the wire to prevent further damage had, inadvertently, set the stage for the events that would follow.

The first mate, stepping in to take control, tried to regain some semblance of order by hauling in slack from the No. 3 wire. But he was also caught by surprise, realizing too late that the vessel was rapidly moving forward. The slack in the wire, accumulated over time as the ship surged, must have been considerable enough to draw the first mate's attention. And though the sailor insisted that he hadn't touched the control lever after starting the winch motor, the fact that the slack had built up so quickly suggests that the wire had been unspooling for a significant period before the first mate took over.

When the *Jupiter* began its forward surge, momentum carried the ship with unexpected force. The No. 4 mooring wire, which had been holding fast, was suddenly taut—an almost mechanical response to the ship's new direction. But the force on the wire was too much for the pile it was anchored to, and the No. 4 mooring pile gave way. The sailor operating the aft winch controls had no time to respond. Had he been able to release some of the tension on the No. 3 wire and adjust the No. 4 wire, perhaps the pile would have held. The key to mitigating the shock-loading, the violent force exerted on the pile, lay in a careful management of the winches. But the sailor, by focusing too much on one line and not adjusting both, allowed the forces to escalate beyond control.

The failure of the No. 4 mooring pile marked the beginning of a cascade of failures.[11] As the pile gave way, the No. 2 mooring wire, now under far more strain than it was designed to bear, took the brunt of the vessel's forward movement. The wire was constrained only by the friction in the winch brake, and it was no match for the ship's momentum. The strain on the No. 2 wire became unbearable. It was the final misstep in a series of miscalculations—each one compounding the other, until the entire system gave way.

The investigation was complicated further by the tragic death of Thomas Sexton, the sailor operating the No. 2 winch. Without his testimony, the NTSB could only speculate on the precise actions he had taken. However, a critical detail remained: When investigators found the No. 1 winch in the payout position and the No. 2 winch in the heave position, they realized that the control settings may have been left that way by the deceased sailor. And while the specifics remained unclear, the configuration of the winches told a broader story of a crew in the midst of a desperate struggle to regain control.

The No. 2 mooring wire, acting as a spring line (controlling forward and backward movement), had been secured to the same pile cluster as the *Jupiter*'s bow. As the ship surged forward, this spring line acted as a lever, causing the stern to swing outward into the river. This uncontrolled motion—a final pivot—was the product of a system designed to hold fast but unable to cope with the overwhelming forces acting upon it.

When the third mate assigned his crew to the winch controls, he wasn't just giving orders. He was trusting them to navigate the delicate balance of anticipation and precision required to manage the movement of the *Jupiter* as the *Buffalo* passed. The winches, particularly the constant-tension types, were designed to hold the vessel steady, absorbing the hydrodynamic forces generated by the larger ship's wake. But in an environment where every moment counts, the crew's response wasn't as refined as it needed to be.

The third mate's expectation was simple: start the winch motors, adjust the wires if necessary, and hold the vessel in place. But what the crew didn't anticipate—or perhaps didn't fully appreciate—was the delicate line between controlling the vessel and inadvertently undermining the winches' purpose. By releasing the brakes on the winches without making the necessary adjustments to the cables, they effectively disengaged the equipment's ability to do its job. The result was a vessel that surged violently at its berth when the *Buffalo* passed, despite the crew's best efforts. The safety board concluded that the crew's handling of the winches was a missed opportunity to use the equipment more effectively, leaving the vessel vulnerable to forces it could have withstood with better preparation.[12]

In the moments leading up to the *Buffalo*'s approach, the crew of the *Jupiter* were preparing for the inevitable—a reaction to the hydrodynamic forces that would soon be exerted on their vessel. The precautions they took were standard practice: They stopped the cargo pumps, started the hydraulic pump for the hose winch, and manned the winch controls, all in anticipation of the *Buffalo*'s wake. The third mate, ever the seasoned watch officer, explained that this routine was familiar—understood by the crew even though it wasn't explicitly written in the *Jupiter*'s operating manual. It was a protocol that had been learned through experience.

But the crew's precautions, though reasonable, weren't enough. They had overlooked key steps that could have minimized the risk. Closing the manifold valve and ullage pipe covers and shutting the motor-operated valve on the pier were critical precautions that weren't taken. Had those valves been closed, the rupture of the cargo hose would have resulted in a far less damaging spill. But with time running out, these additional measures were likely too much to execute before the incident unfolded. And once the fire ignited, any hope of closing those valves disappeared entirely.

The NTSB's recommendation was clear: Cleveland Tankers Inc. needed to include specific procedures in its fleet manuals to address the risks of passing vessels.[13] It wasn't just about stopping cargo operations when another ship was in the vicinity; it was about closing valves, securing ullage covers, and taking every step possible to contain spillage. In a situation like this, preparation isn't just about being ready for the expected—it's about being ready for what might be overlooked in the chaos of the moment.

Meanwhile, as the *Buffalo* neared the entrance of the Saginaw River, the first mate, ever vigilant, had taken the necessary precautions to communicate with nearby vessels.[14] He made a security call on VHF-FM radio channel 16, alerting other marine traffic to the ship's position and its destination. But his awareness didn't stop there. After making the call, he reached out to Station Saginaw River to check the river's height, another routine measure to ensure the ship's safe passage. The interaction was a microcosm of the careful navigation required in busy waterways—ensuring not only that the ship was seen, but also that the ship understood its environment. Later, as the *Buffalo* entered the river, Station Saginaw River made contact again, clarifying the ship's intentions. The Buffalo's master responded, making another security call to reaffirm the freighter's position and destination. These calls were more than just routine—they were an effort to ensure that everyone in the vicinity understood the ship's movements, an effort that might have seemed mundane but was crucial to ensuring the ship's safe passage.

The *Jupiter*'s crew, moored at the Total Petroleum terminal, was not accustomed to monitoring the VHF-FM radio or manning the bridge while stationary. Their focus was on the task at hand—the cargo transfer. This division of responsibilities meant that the third mate, tasked with overseeing the ship's operations, was oblivious to the approach of the *Buffalo* until it was nearly upon them. He first became aware of the looming danger when he heard the *Buffalo*'s whistle requesting the opening of the Independence Bridge and saw the vessel gliding past the D&M railroad bridge.

In those crucial moments, the crew had their attention firmly on the cargo operation. The ship, after all, was at a standstill, and the bustle of the terminal provided a cocoon of activity that, in hindsight, might have shielded them from noticing the *Buffalo* until it was too late. The whistle, a loud and unmistakable signal, was their first clue. Had the *Buffalo*'s captain chosen a less conspicuous means of communication, such as a radio call to the bridge, the crew might have missed the warning altogether. The safety board concluded that the *Jupiter*'s practices were insufficient.[15] The personnel aboard, along with the terminal staff, were not afforded enough time to react and implement safety measures to protect against such risks. There was, in essence, no system in place that guaranteed the crew would know in time when a large vessel was approaching, leaving them vulnerable.

Meanwhile, across the river, the radio watch stander at Station Saginaw River had been aware of the *Buffalo*'s movements. With a simple call, the station could have alerted the Total Petroleum terminal, giving the *Jupiter*'s crew the vital heads-up they needed to begin shutting down operations. But the Coast Guard, though aware of the infrequent large vessel transits, did not require such communications as part of its standard protocol. The NTSB saw an opportunity for improvement here: A simple mandate for vessels to report their movements would have allowed the Coast Guard to act as a sort of conduit, notifying nearby terminals and ensuring that those vessels could prepare for the inevitable.[16] It was a small change that, had it been in place, could have averted disaster.

This is where the need for foresight comes into play. The safety board had already recommended that tank vessels like the *Jupiter*, moored at the Total Petroleum terminal, take additional precautions while discharging cargo—precautions that depended on receiving timely notifications about approaching vessels. But these protocols were only as effective as the information the crew received. In an ideal world, the crew of the *Jupiter* would have known the *Buffalo* was coming, and they would have been able to react in time. Instead, they were caught off guard.

The journey of the *Buffalo* down the Saginaw River offers a glimpse into the uncertainty of those moments. The records detailing its passage were sparse, and the speed at which it moved, though crucial, was left uncalculated at key moments. According to the *Buffalo*'s logbook, it passed the entrance channel range at 8 a.m. and reached the Midland Contracting pier at 9:20 a.m. Station Saginaw River's records noted that the vessel passed the station at 8:15 a.m. But these records didn't provide a complete picture.

Investigators pieced together the puzzle by analyzing the bridgetender's time logs, which tracked the opening and closing of the Independence Bridge. From there, they calculated the *Buffalo*'s average speed. Over the course of its 6.5-mile journey, the *Buffalo* averaged 4.8 knots (5.5 mph), but its speed varied across different segments of the river. Between the river entrance and the D&M railroad bridge, it moved faster, at 5.4 knots (6.2 mph), and by the time it passed the *Jupiter*, its speed had dropped to 4.2 knots (4.8 mph). This estimation was based on the calculated time it took the vessel to cover the 0.7-mile stretch between the D&M railroad bridge and the Independence Bridge.

But there were still questions about the *Buffalo*'s precise speed when it passed the *Jupiter*. The *Buffalo*'s master, upon sighting the *Jupiter* near the railroad bridge, made a critical decision: He adjusted the vessel's propeller pitch to four feet, the minimum setting that still allowed him to maintain control. He admitted, however, that he didn't fully understand how pitch correlated to speed, especially in the context of the Saginaw River. This was a moment of uncertainty, a gap in the information that the master needed to navigate the vessel with precision. Investigators, too, found it difficult to confirm the *Buffalo*'s exact speed as it passed the *Jupiter*, since the Buffalo didn't maintain pitch-to-speed records during river passages. The *Buffalo*'s approach was a moment of fine margins—one in which the smallest of miscalculations or misunderstandings about speed and control could lead to catastrophic consequences.

Ultimately, the NTSB found that the breakdown wasn't just a result of a single misstep, but a series of missed opportunities—both for the crew of the *Jupiter* and the Coast Guard.[17] What could have been a routine transit became a tragedy due to a failure in communication, a lack of preparation, and the absence of a system that would have ensured safety at every stage. The question, then, is not just what happened, but why. And, perhaps more importantly, what can be done to ensure that such oversights never happen again.

The *Buffalo*'s master and chief engineer both testified that the four-foot pitch setting was the lowest the propeller could go before reaching zero pitch—a setting that would have rendered the vessel uncontrollable. In their minds, this was the crucial threshold. Yet, while the safety board was confident that the

Buffalo was indeed set to a four-foot pitch when it passed the *Jupiter*, it were unable to pinpoint whether the vessel had slowed down enough by that point to align with the corresponding speed.

There was another element at play: wind. The *Buffalo*'s master explained that due to the wind pushing against the vessel's starboard side, he was forced to steer closer to the *Jupiter* than he normally would have. His goal was simple: avoid drifting toward the opposite bank. In doing so, he believed he had passed the *Jupiter* with a clearance of approximately sixty to sixty-five feet, a figure that the *Jupiter*'s crew members corroborated. This clearance, while close, was still within the bounds of what the master deemed acceptable. But, as with many things in life, the devil is in the details. The *Jupiter*'s port side extended beyond but remained close to the western edge of the two-hundred-foot-wide channel, while the centerline of the *Buffalo*, at sixty-eight feet in beam, was nearly at the heart of the channel.

Now, imagine the scene. The *Buffalo*'s master, an experienced ship handler, understood the dynamics of the waterway. He knew steering any closer to the eastern edge of the channel would have risked grounding the vessel. But what struck the NTSB was his claim that he had passed "closer than normal" to the *Jupiter*, all due to the wind. This was a subtle yet telling admission.[18]

If you dig deeper, you realize that, when the master navigated vessels past the Total Petroleum terminal, he typically aimed for a greater distance from the moored vessels, steering closer to the opposite bank. The problem, however, is that by passing the *Jupiter* at this reduced distance, he unintentionally increased the hydrodynamic forces acting on the ship, forces that the *Jupiter*—moored so tightly—could not withstand.[19]

At this point, the question becomes clear: Could this have been avoided? Yes. Had the master reduced speed, the hydrodynamic forces would have been minimized. And if reducing speed wasn't possible, he could have increased his distance from the *Jupiter*, giving the moored vessel more space to absorb those forces without surging. By failing to do both, the *Buffalo*'s proximity and speed combined in a way that caused the *Jupiter* to surge heavily at the berth, ultimately leading to the breakaway.

Now, consider the mate on watch aboard the *Buffalo*, whose primary duty was to observe the wake. It's easy to imagine how, with limited responsibilities, the mate could have recorded the times the vessel passed buoys and bridges. But the regulations that govern large and powerful vessel like the Buffalo require much more than mere observation. Under Coast Guard regulations, vessels over 1,600 gross tons are mandated to record their position on navigation charts and to adjust their speed based on factors such as under-keel clearance, wake damage, and any local speed restrictions. These are not optional steps; they are part of the fundamental discipline of navigation.

Why does this matter? The large vessels of the Great Lakes, including the *Buffalo*, should be continuously aware of their position, speed, and the consequences of their movements, especially when passing other vessels moored in narrow, congested waterways. Keeping accurate records of engine maneuvers and courses steered—whether manually or automatically—could have made a world of difference in the *Buffalo* incident. These records would have provided essential insights for investigators, helping to reconstruct the vessel's track and giving a clearer picture of the sequence of events. More importantly, if the *Buffalo*'s speed had been a safety concern, these records would have shown when and how the ship adjusted its pace.

The safety board's recommendation was clear: Bridge watch crews aboard vessels over 1,600 gross tons should keep detailed logs of their vessel's position at regular intervals, document engine maneuvers, and record compass headings.[20] In doing so, they would gain a heightened awareness of the risks involved in navigating these massive ships through narrow channels. It's not just about managing speed—it's about understanding the impact of that speed on the environment around you, from the wake you leave behind to the forces you impose on other vessels. Keeping track of every turn and every shift in speed is not just good practice; it's essential to avoiding the type of collision and breakaway that occurred between the *Buffalo* and the *Jupiter*.

Total Petroleum's approach to inspecting its Bay City pier was marked by a series of oversights that, in hindsight, seem almost inevitable. Their inspections—periodic as they were—did not go beyond a cursory visual assessment of the mooring piles. A marine construction company had conducted an inspection, but crucially, it failed to probe or test the integrity of the piles beyond their surface appearance. The marine contractor missed signs that would later become central to the investigation—the subtle rot within the wood that, although not immediately obvious, was critical for the safe mooring of a vessel like the *Jupiter*.

The wood, once analyzed by a USDA laboratory, revealed its weakness. In truth, it wasn't strong enough to secure a vessel of such size—especially one that could be affected by the immense hydrodynamic forces generated by a passing ship. Yet, because the *Jupiter* was a large vessel and only berthed at the Bay City terminal sporadically, Total Petroleum had more than enough time to carry out a thorough inspection and initiate repairs without disrupting normal operations.

But here's where things get troubling. The marine contractor, tasked with ensuring the pier's integrity, didn't just overlook one small detail—it missed the center pile in the No. 4 pile cluster entirely during the most recent inspection. And this pile wasn't just any pile; it was the key to securing the *Jupiter*.[21] It was the primary support that held the vessel in place. Had Total Petroleum carried out a more diligent inspection, the rot would likely have been spotted in time for repairs, sparing the company—and everyone involved—a much more costly and dangerous incident.

The NTSB's verdict was clear: Total Petroleum's failure to properly maintain and inspect the mooring facilities was a clear case of negligence.[22] The company should have implemented more rigorous and regular surveys of the mooring piles, with a special focus on the center pile, the most crucial element in ensuring a vessel's safety. And this lack of attention to detail did not stop there. As the accident unfolded, gasoline spilled onto the pier from a broken nitrogen purge line connection on the twelve-inch pipeline.

This alone might have been dangerous, but it wasn't until sparks from the damaged electrical conduit ignited the fuel that the situation escalated. The fire quickly spread to the *Jupiter*, igniting gasoline leaking from the ruptured cargo hose. The fire spread rapidly across the midship area and around the open ullage pipes, which were intended to provide a safe means of venting but, in this case, played a dangerous role in the fire's escalation.

The design flaw in the ullage pipes was a critical factor. The inner periphery of the ullage pipes lacked a continuous shoulder or ledge to properly support the flame screens, which were supposed to act as a barrier against flames. This created a gap wide enough for a measuring tape to be inserted without removing the screen, rendering the flame screens ineffective. While these flame screens met the Coast Guard's regulatory standards, the way they were installed made them virtually useless in this situation.[23] And here's the irony: this was a design flaw that, according to a Coast Guard spokesman, should have been caught through "common sense" during routine inspections. But it wasn't, and the gap between the screen's edge and the pipe allowed the fire to spread unchecked.

The *Jupiter* incident, in a way, exemplifies how a series of small oversights—things that might seem insignificant at the time—can compound into a disaster.

Total Petroleum's failure to properly inspect and maintain the mooring piles combined with a regulatory loophole in the installation of flame screens to set the stage for the catastrophe. What seems like a chain of unrelated mistakes is actually a case study in how systemic failures at multiple levels—both operational and regulatory—can combine to produce a catastrophic result.

In the wake of the *Jupiter* incident, the safety board issued a clear recommendation to the Coast Guard: Inspectors must rigorously examine the installation of flame screens, ensuring that they fully seal the openings around their periphery.[24] This, the board argued, could prevent a situation like the one that unfolded on the *Jupiter*, where improperly installed flame screens allowed a fire on deck to spread into the cargo tanks, leading to a catastrophic explosion. But there was another layer to the disaster: Had the crew closed the ullage pipe covers when the *Jupiter* stopped discharging, allowing the tanks to vent safely through the pressure/vacuum valves, it's likely that the explosions could have been avoided altogether. The fire might have been contained using the fixed-foam extinguishing system before the heat had a chance to ignite the vapors inside the tanks.

This is where the *Jupiter*'s disaster becomes a poignant reminder of the delicate balance between small decisions and catastrophic outcomes. The NTSB's investigation pinpointed the most likely cause of the explosions: the fire's spread through the open ullage pipes due to the flame screens' faulty installation. This was not just an issue of negligence—it was a systemic failure to account for how one design flaw could trigger a chain reaction of events, ultimately leading to disaster.

Total Petroleum's operating manual, approved by the Coast Guard, detailed the necessary procedures for handling liquid petroleum products safely. It outlined the hazards, provided instructions for spill response, and included contact information for agencies to notify in case of an emergency. However, one glaring omission stood out: The manual did not specify what terminal employees should do when a berthed vessel was engaged in transfer operations and was approached by another large vessel.[25]

This lack of clarity left decisions in the hands of the vessel personnel, who, in this case, did not suspend operations when it would have been prudent to do so. The safety board contended that Total Petroleum should have played a more active role in overseeing the safety of such operations, especially given the potential risks posed by passing river traffic. A simple provision in the manual to notify berthed vessels when large vessels were expected to pass through the waterway could have allowed crews to pause operations in advance—mitigating the risk of a surge.

This gap in the manual wasn't just an oversight—it was a blind spot in the safety framework that should have been addressed. While the Coast Guard had inspected Total Petroleum's operations and approved the manual, confirming its compliance with existing regulations, the manual's failure to address situations like passing vessels represented a missed opportunity to enhance safety. The NTSB recommended that the Coast Guard revise its regulations to include specific shutdown procedures when passing vessels posed a risk of surging.[26] In doing so, both terminal operators and vessel crews would share the responsibility for safety—an essential step toward reducing the risk of pollution and casualties in these high-stakes environments.

But the issues at Total Petroleum didn't stop with the manual. The terminal manager, seated in his office when the *Buffalo* sounded its whistle, was unaware of the approaching vessel. Despite having a VHF-FM radio in the office, it was set to the frequency used by the terminal operator and the watch officer aboard the *Jupiter*, not the one used for general communications with passing vessels. As a result, the manager did not receive the critical early warning that could have allowed terminal personnel to prepare for the incoming traffic. While shoreside facilities were not required to monitor VHF-FM channel 16, this failure to stay informed about approaching vessels illustrated how small gaps in communication can have significant consequences.

Had the terminal been alerted in advance—perhaps by the Coast Guard—about the incoming *Buffalo*, personnel could have taken appropriate precautions. The lack of communication between the terminal and the vessel crew, particularly during transfer operations, was a significant risk factor. Early notification of an approaching vessel would have given terminal personnel the time to assess the situation, inform the berthed vessel, and potentially suspend transfer operations before the hazard could escalate.

What we see in this series of events is a chain of failures, each building on the one before it—small lapses in judgment, communication, and procedure that together created a perfect storm. In hindsight, the solutions seem simple: better inspection of flame screens, clear procedures for managing passing traffic, and enhanced communication between vessel and terminal staff. But in the moment, these were details that went overlooked. The safety board's recommendations, if implemented, would provide a much-needed safety net—a framework for anticipating and preventing similar incidents in the future.

Imagine for a moment that the terminal manager at Total Petroleum had been given a clear, early warning about the *Buffalo*'s approach. The entire sequence of events could have unfolded differently. Early awareness would have allowed the terminal manager to alert the *Jupiter*'s watch officer well before the situation escalated. Simple, proactive communication—telling the watch officer about the oncoming vessel—could have been the key to averting a disaster.

It's not just about the notification; it's about the critical tasks that follow: suspending cargo transfer operations, manning mooring winches, and ensuring everything is running smoothly. These tasks shouldn't have been left to chance, yet that's precisely what happened. Terminal personnel had a responsibility to share the burden of keeping the vessels at their facility informed about movements in the river during transfer operations. It wasn't just a matter of convenience but of safety.

The setup was there for a more efficient response: Both the terminal operator and the *Jupiter*'s deck officer had handheld radios tuned to the terminal manager's frequency. With that kind of communication link, the exchange of vital information could have been quick and seamless. The operator, stationed near the vessel, could have immediately passed the message along. But the critical piece—timely communication—was missing. The NTSB noted that an extra precaution would have been to establish a system where terminal personnel received updates from Station Saginaw River, giving them the opportunity to provide timely warnings to the vessels at the pier, thus avoiding the chaos that would ultimately unfold.[27]

When the *Jupiter*'s explosion shattered the calm of the morning, Coast Guard personnel at Station Saginaw River acted swiftly. Within thirteen minutes, they were on scene, racing toward the fire. The proximity of the station to the accident site meant that their response time was lightning fast. But when the Coast Guard personnel arrived, they found themselves in a crisis that exceeded their capabilities. The fire was overwhelming, and while they initially tried to fight the blaze, it became clear they had to shift their focus. The priority, they realized, was to save lives. The Coast Guard team's decision to concentrate on rescuing the crew members in the water, rather than trying to battle a fire they couldn't contain, was the right one. Without their quick and effective response, the death toll could have been far higher. The safety board couldn't have been clearer: The Coast Guard's actions limited the number of fatalities and injuries, and its team's professionalism in the face of chaos should be commended.[28]

In the aftermath, the *Jupiter*'s crew responded with the kind of calm urgency that can only come from proper training. Within minutes of the explosion, the master had notified the Coast Guard and was organizing the crew. Everyone was accounted for on the stern of the vessel, donning life jackets or exposure suits in preparation for abandoning ship. Yet, tragedy still struck. The third mate and another crewman, trapped on the bow, couldn't retrieve life jackets in time. When they jumped overboard, one man drowned. The NTSB speculated that the man who died could have survived had he been able to grab a life jacket before he was forced to jump. In an ideal world, everyone would have been able to evacuate in an orderly, calm fashion. But the unpredictable nature of a shipboard fire meant that the most practical decision was to evacuate as quickly as possible. The *Jupiter*'s master, uncertain whether additional explosions were imminent and seeing that the fixed-foam extinguishing system was compromised, made the difficult but necessary call to order the crew off the ship.

Even with the swift response of local fire and emergency teams, the fire's scale was beyond anything they had been prepared for. Two and a half days of furious, relentless effort—by local firefighters, the Coast Guard, and a commercial firefighting company—finally brought the flames under control. At a December 6 critique, participants reflected on the initial response with surprising honesty, acknowledging that they had simply lacked the equipment and expertise needed to combat a fire of that magnitude. Fires aboard ships, particularly tankships, were rare in the Bay City/Saginaw River area. But the *Jupiter* disaster illuminated a clear need: Local fire departments had to receive specialized training in shipboard firefighting. Without it, they were playing catch-up, and lives were on the line.

This sequence of events is a case study in how a breakdown in communication, lack of preparation, and insufficient training can lead to a cascade of preventable problems. The *Jupiter*'s crew acted swiftly under pressure, but they were not the only ones who could have prevented the fire from spreading. The safety board's recommendations—improved communication protocols, better training for first responders, a more proactive approach to vessel safety—point to a future where such disasters are less likely.[29] It's not just about responding in the moment; it's about preparing, anticipating, and addressing gaps before tragedy strikes.

In the aftermath of the explosion, the Coast Guard units from Station Saginaw River swiftly swung into action, deploying oil booms to contain the environmental damage. The Coast Guard district commander, mindful of the magnitude of the disaster, also provided the buoy tender *Bramble* as a platform for commercial firefighters who battled the relentless fire. Yet, the incident laid bare a critical gap in the Bay City area's emergency preparedness: While there was a contingency plan in place, it lacked provisions for handling shipboard fires or other marine disasters of this scale.

The NTSB had already recognized this shortcoming in previous reports, urging the Coast Guard to work more closely with local authorities to develop comprehensive port contingency plans. These plans, the safety board suggested, should involve local waterfront facilities, fire and police departments, port authority agencies, and other disaster preparedness organizations. The idea was straightforward: a more coordinated approach to disaster management, one that would blend the expertise of local responders with the resources of federal agencies. This wasn't a novel concept—back in 1985, following a cruise ship fire in Port Canaveral, Florida, the NTSB had issued a similar recommendation to the Coast Guard.[30] It advocated that all Coast Guard stations implement a robust contingency plan to address such emergencies. The Coast Guard, responding to the recommendation, integrated it into the Marine Safety Manual, instructing the captain of the port (COTP) to create firefighting contingency plans for every port within the COTP's jurisdiction. This, the Coast Guard believed, would close the loop on emergency preparedness, ensuring that local authorities had the resources and training to respond effectively.

The result? Both the Canaveral Port Authority and the Coast Guard saw positive results, with the port authority acquiring emergency equipment and initiating training programs. These actions were classified as "Closed—Acceptable Action" by the safety board. However, for the Bay City/Saginaw River area, the NTSB was clear: The Detroit Coast Guard COTP needed to follow suit and collaborate with local agencies to develop a port-specific contingency plan that included shipboard firefighting training and drills. The incident had exposed how fragile the system was when local preparedness didn't align with the scale of a maritime disaster.[31]

But the gaps in response didn't end there. Another, perhaps subtler, issue emerged in the wake of the explosion: the handling of toxicological testing. Chemical tests for drugs and alcohol are highly time-sensitive, and the Coast Guard regulations were explicit: Marine employers had to ensure that specimens were collected as soon as possible after an incident. Here, the *Jupiter*'s master and operator were understandably consumed by the immediate need to rescue the crew and manage the chaos of the situation. Their focus, rightfully, was on survival. However, the responsibility to collect toxicological samples remained.

The crew's failure to secure those samples in a timely manner became a pivotal oversight. While it's clear that the crew's actions in the immediate aftermath were focused on life-saving efforts, the regulations on toxicological testing were just as critical for determining the circumstances surrounding the accident. The safety board noted that the operator and master should have notified the hospital to collect specimens from the injured crew members who were transported there. Meanwhile, the uninjured crew should have been tested as soon as the emergency conditions stabilized. But because the specimens weren't collected until the following day, meaningful alcohol testing became impossible.[32]

The timeline of events reveals the challenges in balancing immediate crisis management with the longer-term procedural requirements. The explosion occurred at 8:35 a.m., but the *Buffalo* crew didn't initially recognize their involvement. It wasn't until later that afternoon that a Coast Guard officer informed the *Buffalo*'s master of the ship's role in the accident and the need to collect specimens. By then, some of the crew had already gone ashore, complicating the process. It wasn't until 7 p.m. that the marine employer collected urine specimens from nine crew members, but the window for meaningful alcohol testing had long passed.

The NTSB argued that the moment the Coast Guard arrived aboard the *Buffalo*, they should have taken immediate action, instructing the master to collect urine specimens on the spot. Had they done so, alcohol testing might have been possible, offering crucial insight into whether it played a role in the accident. This wasn't just a regulatory lapse; it was a missed opportunity to gather vital evidence that could have painted a clearer picture of what led to the explosion.

In both the response to the fire and the handling of the toxicological testing, the *Jupiter* incident exposed a series of procedural gaps and missed opportunities. Each of these elements—the firefighting training, the coordination with local agencies, and the toxicological testing—highlight the intricacies of emergency preparedness in the maritime world. What seems like a small misstep—failing to take a timely sample or neglecting a single piece of training—can have far-reaching consequences. It's a reminder that in crisis management, the devil truly is in the details.

The NTSB found itself in a peculiar situation during its investigation. While the Medical Review Officer (MRO) for each ship had provided an assessment of the toxicological test results for the *Buffalo* and *Jupiter* crew members, the actual laboratory data remained elusive. The MROs' reports didn't mention when the specimens had been collected or which drugs were included in the testing protocols. When investigators consulted with experts to interpret the results, it became clear: Alcohol testing had not been conducted, and the MROs themselves weren't even aware whether such tests had been performed. This gap in the testing procedures became a significant concern.

The MRO report for the *Buffalo* claimed that its crew "met the drug-free requirements specified under U.S. Coast Guard regulations." Similarly, the report for the *Jupiter*'s crew indicated they had "undergone a substance abuse test in accordance with applicable Department of Transportation regulations." But here's where things get complicated: Neither report mentioned alcohol testing, which, according to the safety board, was a critical part of the required substance abuse testing. And so, the NTSB disagreed with the assertion that the crew members had undergone a fully compliant substance abuse test as stipulated by regulations.

The concern, it seemed, wasn't just about regulatory compliance; it was about the practical impact of the delay. Toxicological testing had not been conducted promptly, which meant the opportunity for effective alcohol testing was lost. And in a case where the cause of the disaster was so unclear, testing for alcohol could have provided the critical clues needed to piece the puzzle together. The safety board also noted that the MROs' reports could have been misleading, as they did not fully address the failure to carry out proper alcohol testing.

Meanwhile, the investigation into the *Buffalo* and its actions in relation to the *Jupiter* also raised questions. The *Buffalo* was reported to have been moving with a four-foot pitch as it passed the *Jupiter*, but due to the absence of engine maneuvering records, investigators could not pin down the exact speed. The lack of this data was a frustrating gap in the investigation, especially since the *Buffalo*'s speed and proximity created powerful hydrodynamic forces that led to the *Jupiter* surging against the pier. The surge broke the No. 4 mooring pile and caused the ship to swing into the river, rupturing the flexible discharge hose in the process.

And then there was the failure of the mooring system itself. Total Petroleum's Bay City terminal only had four mooring devices, a number that proved insufficient to secure a large vessel like the *Jupiter*. The crew of the *Jupiter*, spotting the *Buffalo*'s approach, tried to act quickly. They stopped the cargo pumps and activated the constant-tension winches in an effort to minimize the impact of the hydrodynamic forces. But with little time, they couldn't take all necessary precautions, such as closing the ullage covers and discharge valves.

The *Jupiter* crew, for all their efforts, were blindsided by the absence of an alert system. They had no warning of the *Buffalo*'s approach on the Saginaw River, leaving them to react in the moment rather than proactively adjust to the risk. Their reaction was further hindered by mechanical failures: The No. 3 wire cable, for instance, was unable to prevent the ship from surging backward because the winch motor's brake had released. And when the ship surged forward, the No. 4 mooring pile was subjected to a shock load, leading to its failure.

The repercussions were catastrophic. Sparks from damaged electrical conduits ignited the gasoline that had spilled on the pier, triggering a fire that spread quickly to the *Jupiter*'s deck. Explosions followed when the flames traveled through improperly installed flame screens in the open ullage pipes and reached the cargo tanks. It was a chain reaction that could have been avoided with more robust systems and procedures.

As the investigation continued, the NTSB uncovered more failures.[33] The *Jupiter*'s operating manual was inadequate, lacking specific instructions on how to respond to surging caused by a passing vessel's wake. A ship's operating manual is crucial in setting the standard for crew preparedness, yet this one fell short when it came to outlining how to handle such dynamic and dangerous situations.

The fire aboard the *Jupiter* burned for two and a half days before a commercial firefighting team was able to extinguish it. During that time, local firefighters, although well intentioned, lacked the training and equipment necessary to combat a shipboard fire of this magnitude. The disaster contingency plan for the Saginaw River/Bay City area, similarly, was found to be inadequate. It didn't account for shipboard fire training for local departments, leaving a major gap in regional preparedness. And then there was the issue of post-accident drug and alcohol testing, which had not been properly followed. The timeline of events, coupled with the lack of proper procedures, highlighted just how the failure to adhere to protocols could have delayed or even sabotaged the investigation into what caused the disaster.

In its final analysis, the NTSB concluded that the fire and explosions aboard the *Jupiter* were primarily caused by Total Petroleum's failure to provide adequate mooring facilities.[34] This failure allowed the vessel to break free when a passing ship's wake caused surging, setting off a series of unfortunate events. Contributing factors included poor crew procedures for managing mooring lines and winches, and the *Buffalo*'s decision to navigate too close to the *Jupiter*. The severity of the incident was further exacerbated by the lack of an alert system for the *Jupiter*'s crew, and the failure of both the *Jupiter*'s owners and the U.S. Coast Guard to ensure the proper installation of flame screens.

The safety board's recommendations were sweeping and aimed at improving safety and preparedness at every level—from the Coast Guard to the individual companies involved.[35] The U.S. Coast Guard was urged to implement specific procedures in Facility Operating Manuals, ensuring that product transfers could be halted when surging from passing vessels posed a risk. The Coast Guard was also instructed to improve communication systems between its stations and local facilities, ensuring that alerts about passing vessels were communicated in a timely manner. Total Petroleum, too, was called to task, with instructions to enhance its inspection protocols and shore up mooring facilities to ensure they could handle vessels of varying sizes. Even Cleveland Tankers, responsible for operating the *Jupiter*, was urged to revise its fleet manuals to include procedures for suspending cargo transfers during potentially hazardous conditions.

In the wake of the investigation, a single, undeniable truth emerged: Safety in the maritime industry is as much about preparation as it is about response. Each gap, each oversight, compounded the disaster. The NTSB's recommendations, if followed, could help prevent the next tragedy. But the question remained: Would they be heeded?

CHAPTER 6

Lessons Learned

ON DECEMBER 3, 1991, OVER A YEAR AFTER THE DISASTER, A SMALL GROUP OF FEDERAL investigators sat down to answer a very large question: *What do you do after a catastrophe?* The National Transportation Safety Board, acting in its role as the nation's conscience of accident and error, began issuing its findings on the disaster of the *Jupiter*. And what's striking is not just who the NTSB blamed, but how carefully it parceled out responsibility. One recommendation went to Bay County. Another to the Michigan State Police Emergency Management Division. Still another to the Lake Carriers' Association. Cleveland Tankers, the company at the center of the story, received two. Total Petroleum, four. And the U.S. Coast Guard—perhaps the only institution with both the reach and the authority to make sweeping change—received six.

To the Michigan State Police Emergency Management Division, the NTSB's advice was simple: revise the workbook.[1] The agency's county emergency planning manual was a binder of procedures—step-by-step guides for what to do in the event of chemical leaks, tornadoes, or power outages. What it did not contain, somewhat remarkably, were instructions on how to fight a fire aboard a ship. So the safety board asked the agency to amend the workbook to include provisions for shipboard firefighting training and procedures for marine fires.

The state police organization, to its credit, responded. It promised to fix the omission, and in April of 1998, nearly seven years after the *Jupiter* went up in flames, it mailed the NTSB a copy of the newly printed manual.[2] The case was closed. The state police actions, the board decided, were "acceptable."

Bay County was a different story. To the county, the NTSB made a similar request: update the county's emergency contingency plan to include guidelines for shipboard fires.[3] But Bay County never answered. Not in 1993 when the board asked, not later that summer when the request was repeated, not even after the case was officially closed in 1994.[4] The silence was complete.

The irony, of course, is that on the night of the explosion, everyone—Bay County, the Coast Guard, the local fire departments—had responded as best they could. Within minutes of the blast, the ship's master, Beckwith, had ordered a head count on the stern. The first mate had ensured that every man there had either a life jacket or an exposure suit. And when it became clear that the fire was beyond their ability to fight, Beckwith gave the order to abandon ship. Two crew members, Rentschler and Sexton, were trapped on the bow and forced to leap into the water without life jackets, but for the rest of the crew, the evacuation was as orderly as such things can be. It was the right decision: The fixed-foam extinguishing system had failed, and no one knew if more explosions were imminent.

Onshore, the response followed the same logic. The fire departments let the blaze burn. Not because they wanted to, but because—as they later admitted in a meeting at Bay City Hall—there was no equipment, no training, no capacity to do otherwise.[5] The Coast Guard provided platforms, booms, and logistics. A commercial firefighting company was eventually brought in. And still it took two and a half days before the fire was fully extinguished.

Shipboard fires might be rare in Bay City, but rarity is not the same as impossibility. In the wake of the *Jupiter* disaster, therefore, the NTSB focused on something that seemed, at first glance, almost trivial: recordkeeping. The safety board recommended that the Lake Carriers' Association establish a procedure—manual or automatic—for logging engine maneuvers whenever one of its vessels entered or left port, or at any other moment when careful handling mattered most.[6]

Why? Because the *Buffalo*, a massive freighter, had left behind a curious absence of data. Its logbook noted that it passed the channel marker at 8:00 a.m. and that it arrived at the Midland pier an hour and twenty minutes later. But between those two points, there was nothing—no record of speed, no times at bridges or landmarks. The Coast Guard's station logs filled in a single gap (the vessel passed the station at 8:15), but otherwise investigators were left to reconstruct the *Buffalo*'s passage like detectives solving a crime without witnesses.[7]

When the ship's master was asked what speed he carried past the *Jupiter*, he explained that he had set his pitch to four feet—the minimum he believed necessary to maintain control in the Saginaw River. But he admitted he had no idea what speed that setting translated to.[8] Pitch, after all, is not speed; it is simply the angle of the propeller blade in the water. Investigators eventually estimated that the *Buffalo* was moving at roughly 4.2 knots (about 4.8 mph) when it passed. Not fast by highway standards, but in the constrained geometry of a two-hundred-foot-wide channel alongside a moored tanker, speed behaves differently.

Hydrodynamics is invisible until it isn't. A large vessel moving through confined water creates forces that can tug at nearby ships, pulling them toward its wake. On that morning, the *Buffalo*'s proximity to the *Jupiter*—just sixty or so feet—meant that the forces of water movement were enough to yank the tanker violently at its berth. The mooring lines snapped. The *Jupiter* broke free. And moments later, the disaster unfolded.

The NTSB's reasoning was straightforward: If vessels kept better records of their speed and engine settings, investigators could reconstruct events more accurately.[9] More importantly, captains and mates would be more aware, in the moment, of just how precarious their maneuvers were. It was about cultivating a culture of awareness.

The Lake Carriers' Association, however, saw the matter differently. In its response, it rejected the recommendation outright.[10] Logging maneuvers, the association argued, would do nothing to prevent accidents. At best, the log would provide data for future investigators. The real cause, it insisted, was the poor mooring facilities at the Total Petroleum dock. Anything else, the association said, was a distraction—a "nice to have," not essential.

The NTSB disagreed. It pointed out that continuous recording of engine maneuvers was standard practice in much of the maritime world. It was not an academic exercise but a discipline, a way to make ships safer and crews more accountable. "It is recognized as a critical element in the efficient, safe, and disciplined operation of these ships," the safety board wrote in reply.[11] But the Lake Carriers' Association refused to budge. "Vessels in the Great Lakes would not gain any significant benefit," it wrote, dismissing the idea as bureaucratic overreach.[12] In November 1992, the file was closed: *unacceptable action.*[13]

The irony is hard to miss. The *Buffalo* had passed the *Jupiter* at a speed its captain couldn't quite name, with forces he couldn't quite see, leaving behind a logbook that told investigators almost nothing. In a world defined by steel, horsepower, and precision, the accident hinged not just on the physics of water but on the absence of something as mundane as a written record.

When the NTSB turned its attention to Total Petroleum, the list of recommendations the safety board produced was surprisingly practical. There was nothing abstract about them, no grand pronouncements on policy or regulation. Instead, they read almost like housekeeping instructions: Make sure vessels moored at the dock have both fore and aft leads for their bow and stern lines. Create a procedure for receiving traffic updates from the Coast Guard and pass that information to the ships tied up at the terminal. Amend the operating manual to spell out when to halt loading and unloading if passing traffic could make the docked vessels surge. And, finally, test the pilings—poke at the wood every year to see if it has grown soft with age.[14]

The recommendations might seem almost mundane. But hidden in their simplicity was the central lesson of the *Jupiter* disaster: that catastrophe is rarely the result of one catastrophic mistake. More often, it is the accumulation of small oversights—weak moorings, missing signals, out-of-date manuals—that, when stacked together, make disaster inevitable.

To its credit, Total Petroleum responded with more than just compliance. In rebuilding its dock facility, the company replaced the fragile wooden pilings with steel pipes filled with concrete—structures designed not just for the ships that had always come to Bay City, but for vessels larger and smaller that might arrive in the future. It added new moorings, the kind that could support bow and stern lines with proper forward and aft leads.[15] And it rewrote it operating manual. Now, when a vessel approached either the downstream railroad bridge or the upstream Independence Bridge, terminal operators would halt the transfer of petroleum immediately.[16]

It is tempting to see these changes as obvious—what any sensible operator would have done after a tragedy. But hindsight always makes prudence appear inevitable. At the time, each of these details represented a shift: from wooden pilings to steel, from passive to active monitoring, from assuming ships would stay put to preparing for the fact that sometimes they don't. In the end, the lesson wasn't about pilings or mooring lines at all. It was about the quiet, unglamorous discipline of imagining what could go wrong before it does.

The NTSB's recommendations to Cleveland Tankers were, in essence, about tiny gaps—literal gaps. The safety board wanted the company to modify the flame screen installations on its vessels so that each one formed a complete seal around the edge of the pipe.[17] No slivers of space. No wiggle room. Nothing left unaccounted for.

The second recommendation was broader, though just as specific. The company, the NTSB said, needed to spell out in its fleet manuals what to do when another ship passed nearby.[18] Suspend the transfer of hazardous liquids. Shut the valves. Close the ullage covers. Write it down. Make it procedure.

On the morning of the accident, the crew of the *Jupiter* thought they were prepared. They did what they always did when a large vessel approached: They stopped the cargo pumps and started the hydraulic pump for the hose winch. The third mate later explained that these steps weren't in the manual—they were just habits the crew had developed over time. Everyone knew the ship would surge when another freighter went by. Everyone knew you had to brace for it.

But here's the cruel twist: The precautions weren't enough. Had the crew closed the manifold valve and the ullage pipe covers, the explosions might never have occurred. The tanks would have vented through the proper valves, and the spilled gasoline would have been limited to whatever remained in the hose. Instead, when gasoline poured onto the pier and sparks from a damaged electrical conduit found their fuel, fire raced across the deck. Contained by the spill rails, the flames gathered around the ullage pipes. And there, in the most ordinary of oversights, the fire found its way in.

The flame screens had met Coast Guard standards.[19] They were, technically speaking, compliant. But they didn't *fit*. The clearance between the edge of the screen and the pipe was so wide that crew members sometimes tucked a measuring tape into the space without removing the screen. And that was all the fire needed. A narrow path. A gap smaller than the width of a finger. That was how it slipped past the barrier and into the tanks.

In the end, the safety board concluded that this was the most likely cause of the explosions: not negligence in the grand sense, not some spectacular act of error, but the propagation of fire through a design flaw so subtle it was invisible—until it wasn't. Cleveland Tankers, to its credit, responded. The company rewrote its fleet manuals. It adjusted every flame screen.[20] It did what the NTSB asked. But the larger lesson is harder to codify. Safety is not just about rules and compliance. It is about the spaces in between—the margins where human habit meets technical detail, where a half-inch gap can be the difference between a routine transfer of gasoline and a fireball that lights up the river.

For decades, ships had docked at Total Petroleum's Bay City terminal without incident. The pier was old but serviceable, the mooring piles weathered but, in the eyes of inspectors, still sound. The Coast Guard had looked, the ships had tied up, and everything appeared fine. Yet appearances can be deceiving. When one of the wooden mooring piles finally failed, at the worst possible moment, it wasn't because of something visible. It was because of rot—silent, invisible, spreading from the inside out.

The Department of Agriculture lab that tested the failed pile couldn't measure exactly how weak it had become. But the evidence of decay was there. The wood had lost its strength long before anyone realized it. The lesson, the NTSB concluded, was obvious: You can't just look at the surface of wooden pilings. You have to probe them, test them, push past what the eye can see. Safety depends on what's hidden.

Meanwhile, another failure was unfolding on the river itself. As the *Buffalo* steamed toward Bay City, its first mate dutifully announced the vessel's presence over the radio, twice, and checked in with the Coast Guard station at Saginaw River. But the *Jupiter*'s crew never heard the calls. They weren't listening. The ship's bridge was unmanned while the crew focused on cargo transfer, and their operating manual didn't require a radio watch while moored. By the time the third mate noticed the *Buffalo*—by sight, not by sound—it was already passing the railroad bridge.

This was not negligence in the classic sense. It was a blind spot, a hole in practice. If the Coast Guard watch stander, who knew the *Buffalo* was inbound, had simply phoned the terminal, the crew might have had precious minutes to halt operations. If the *Jupiter*'s crew had closed their valves and ullage covers when they stopped discharging, the fire might have stayed on deck. If the flame screens had fit properly, sealing the ullage pipes instead of leaving gaps wide enough to slip a measuring tape through, the fire might never have reached the tanks. But none of those things happened. The small lapses aligned, one after another, into catastrophe.

The Coast Guard's role was both heroic and limited. When the explosions came, its personnel were on scene in just thirteen minutes—fast enough to rescue the crew, too late to contain the fire. They chose to focus on saving lives, a decision the NTSB would later commend as the right one. Still, fighting the fire proved beyond their capability. It took local firefighters, Coast Guard units, and a commercial company two and a half days to finally put it out. In a December meeting afterward, officials admitted they had essentially let the blaze burn itself down. “There was no equipment or trained personnel to extinguish it,” one said.[21]

Six recommendations followed for the Coast Guard.[22] Some were simple—share the lessons of the *Jupiter* more widely, emphasize flame screen inspections, train inspectors to look for gaps. Some were ambitious—develop port contingency plans, integrate drills with local firefighters. A few were resisted. The Coast Guard balked at the idea of calling terminals to warn of vessel traffic, insisting that responsibility lay with the facilities themselves.[23] And when asked to establish industry standards for mooring facilities, the Coast Guard let the matter drop entirely. That file was closed, years later, with the haunting label “unacceptable action.”[24]

But other recommendations did take root. Flame screen standards became a point of emphasis at the Coast Guard’s training school in Yorktown, Virginia.[25] Firefighting contingency plans were revised with help from state fire officials.[26] Pollution prevention regulations were updated to require shutdown procedures when passing vessels posed a risk of surging.[27]

The *Jupiter* disaster, in other words, produced a patchwork legacy: some fixes made, some deferred, some ignored. And that’s the paradox of safety. Everyone sees the fireball. Everyone races to put out the flames. But the real danger—the rotting pile, the unmanned radio, the gap in the flame screen—hides in plain sight, waiting for the moment when all the little failures line up.

In the end, the story of the *Jupiter* is not about fire, or gasoline, or even the physics of hydrodynamic surging. It is about the quiet, unglamorous details that most of us never see. A ship’s logbook. A mooring pile hidden beneath the waterline. A radio call no one heard. A flame screen with a gap small enough to slip a measuring tape through.

The lesson of Bay City is that failure does not announce itself with a single, dramatic act. It accumulates in silence, tucked into routines and assumptions, waiting for the moment when all the small oversights align. And when they do, the result looks like an accident—sudden, violent, inexplicable. But in truth, it is nothing of the sort.

The *Jupiter* disaster reminds us that safety is not the absence of catastrophe; it is the presence of discipline in the margins. It is the willingness to probe the wood for rot, to write down the engine maneuvers, to imagine the unlikely and prepare for it anyway. Catastrophe is built from the ordinary. Which means prevention is, too.

That's the paradox: The difference between routine and disaster often comes down to details so small they are almost invisible. And once you see that, you begin to understand that vigilance isn't heroic. It's humble. It lives in the spaces no one else bothers to look.

Epilogue

WHERE WERE YOU WHEN THE *JUPITER* EXPLODED?

It's a question that followed me throughout my research for this book. But for the people I spoke to, the answers came without hesitation. They were vivid, rooted in the memory of an event that seemed to reach into their very bones.

One man recalled driving home from his job at what was then known as Saginaw Steering Gear, when he saw black smoke rising into the sky. More than thirty miles away, he could already see the flames. As he got closer, his concern deepened. He knew people in the area, and the thought of them in harm's way weighed on him. Others remembered the shock wave, the earth trembling beneath their feet when the massive tanker exploded. It was the kind of thing you don't easily forget—the world shaking, like something cosmic had shifted.

David Van Nostrand, the son of the renowned *Bay City Times* photographer Dick Van Nostrand, was on top of the Independence Bridge that day, camera in hand. "You could feel the heat from the ship as it burned," he told me. The image, seared in his mind, didn't fade even after he returned to college in Big Rapids, more than a hundred miles away. The smoke from the explosion was still visible in the sky there.

Far from the scene, Mike Kajdan was serving in the 82nd Airborne Division in Saudi Arabia as part of Operation Desert Shield when the *Jupiter* disaster struck. "My parents sent me the *Bay City Times* newspaper after it happened," Kajdan said, "but it was over a month before I got it. I still have the paper." For him, the event felt both distant and strangely intimate, as if the explosion were a world away—but also a part of his own experience.

Then there was Brian Martindale, just blocks from the explosion's epicenter. He was asleep in his bed when the blast sent him "literally to the floor." He recalled, "I thought my neighbor's house exploded." The sheer force of the explosion had left him stunned and disoriented, a feeling that's hard to describe unless you've felt it yourself.

Even today, remnants of the *Jupiter*'s legacy linger around Bay City, reminders of that fateful day. At Mulligan's Pub on Center Avenue, a life preserver from the *Jupiter* hangs on the wall. Nearby, the Antique Toy and Firehouse Museum has a dedicated space for the ship, preserving the memory of a disaster that continues to shape the town's history.

But this wasn't just a local event. The *Jupiter*'s explosion reverberated around the world. News of the disaster reached the Soviet Union, making its way into the *Krasnaya Zvezda* (Red Star) newspaper in the September 18 edition. The article, short but striking, offered a stark snapshot: "A powerful explosion occurred aboard the tanker *Jupiter* while it was docked and unloading near Bay City, Michigan. According to the latest reports, 18 crew members were on the burning vessel" (TASS, September 17, 1990).

The *Jupiter* even became the subject of academic inquiry. A graduate engineering class at Detroit's Wayne State University launched their own probe into the explosion, examining everything from its causes to the response—or lack thereof. Using interviews, photographs, and news reports, the class meticulously reconstructed the sequence of events. Some students even chartered planes and boats to get a 360-degree view of the scene, leaving no perspective unexamined. Their investigation illuminated both triumphs and failures. The calm, calculated actions of the on-scene coordinators were lauded as an example of best practices, while the failures—those moments where preventative measures weren't taken—were just as revealing. Many of the class's findings would later echo in the National Transportation Safety Board's own investigations.

Years after the explosion, the *Buffalo*—the ship that had played a pivotal role in the disaster—continued to make headlines. In 1997, ownership of the *Buffalo* returned to the Lawrence Steamship Company, and later that year, the vessel struck the Detroit River Light in Lake Erie, leaving a twenty-five-foot gash in its hull. The ship began taking on water but managed to reach Toledo, Ohio, where it was repaired. Investigators later found that the ship's crew was responsible for the collision. In 2017, the *Buffalo* was sold to Algoma Central Corporation and renamed the *Algoma Buffalo*. Today, the ship continues to ply the Great Lakes, hauling construction materials and road salt, a far cry from its ill-fated days on the Saginaw River.

As for the Total Petroleum site, where the *Jupiter* exploded, it's now a Marathon Petroleum facility. The pier, once used to offload gasoline, hasn't seen a vessel in almost two decades. The last ship to dock there was the *Gemini*—a sister ship to the *Jupiter*. By the time it made its final delivery in October 2006, the *Gemini* had been sold to Algoma and rechristened the *Algosar*.

There is no marker for the ship where it burned. Tours aboard the Bay City Boat Lines vessel the *Princess Wenonah* will bring you within a few feet of where the ship sat, smoldering above the waterline, and a few sentences about its fate. But one could have moved to Bay City in the more than three decades since the *Jupiter* burned and not know of its existence.

So, where were you when the *Jupiter* exploded? For some, the question still lingers. For others, it's an answer that can be recalled in vivid detail. And for the rest of us, it's a lesson in the enduring power of disaster—and the indelible way it marks a community's history.

Acknowledgments

IF THERE'S ONE THING I'VE COME TO REALIZE WHILE WRITING THIS BOOK, IT'S THAT books don't get written by a single person. They're the product of a network—of voices that echo in archives, of conversations over coffee, of the quiet work of librarians and journalists who left breadcrumbs decades earlier. A book, in other words, is less a solitary act of authorship than a collective endeavor. This one is no exception.

My fascination with the Great Lakes began long before I sat down to write these pages. It's hard not to be pulled in—the ships, the wrecks, the half-forgotten stories that hover somewhere between myth and history. What's striking, though, is how much of that allure has been preserved not by official histories, but by the people who cared enough to tell the stories. Writers like Michael Schumacher, Fred Stonehouse, and Ric Mixter don't just document the lakes—they animate them. Schumacher's work on books about Great Lakes vessels made me want to take this project seriously. Stonehouse, with his encyclopedic knowledge, turned ships into characters. And Mixter is one of those people you want to talk to for hours, because his passion is contagious. All three were inspirations for my love of the Great Lakes and, as a result, this endeavor.

This book, in particular, owes an enormous debt to Todd Shorkey. Todd is the sort of person who defies neat description. Yes, he's a firefighter. Yes, he's a captain. He's also a photographer with an uncanny eye for detail. But most of all, Todd is someone who gives freely of himself. When we first connected through Facebook, I had no idea how integral he would become. He opened his logbooks to me, offered photographs that captured more than words could, and lent insights that shaped the very heart of this project. Without Todd, this book looks very different. In fact, it probably doesn't happen at all.

Paul Cormier deserves equal recognition. Imagine sitting across from a man who has lived through one of the central events you're writing about—the *Jupiter* explosion—and who tells his story not with drama but with clarity, generosity, and the easy competence of someone who has spent years in the Coast Guard. That is Paul. His voice helped ground this story in lived experience.

And then there's the Mid-Michigan Antique Toy and Firehouse Museum. One of the central facets of this book is that the story, while documented at the time, is rarely revisited. The lone exception to that is the museum, which dedicates a corner of a room to the *Jupiter*. Walk through its collection, and you're struck by the physicality of memory: a cracked pilothouse window, a steel fragment from the smokestack, a tattered American flag. Each artifact is a reminder that history isn't abstract—it's material, tangible, and often scarred.

The Alice and Jack Wirt Public Library also played an outsized role. Its online archive of *The Bay City Times* became my lifeline. In fact, most of what you read here can be traced back to that resource. And that, of course, leads to the journalists themselves—the reporters and photographers who worked in the chaotic aftermath of the *Jupiter* explosion. They weren't just documenting a fire. They were, in real time, writing the first draft of the history that this book builds upon. Kathy Petersen, Jenni Laidman, Dick Van Nostrand, Michael K. Nowlin, Elizabeth McKenna, Mike Turner, Wes Stafford, Rich Rezler, Ted Kleine, Janice Carrillo, Peter Luke—the list is long, and still incomplete. Their work was meticulous and, in a very real sense, heroic.

I read hundreds of their articles. I sifted through interviews. I combed the National Transportation Safety Board report. And in all of it, one lesson became clear: History is never the work of one person, just as a book is never the work of one author. It's a collaboration across time, between those who lived the story, those who told it first, and those who tell it again.

Notes

Preface

1. Jenni Laidman and Kathy Petersen, "Man Dies as Tanker Explodes," *Bay City Times*, September 17, 1990.
2. Ric Mixter, *The Wheelsmen* (Airworthy Publications, 2009), ix.

Chapter 1. Not Just a River

1. Frank J. Krist and David P. Lusch, "Glacial History of Michigan, U.S.A.: A Regional Perspective," *Developments in Quaternary Science* 2 (2004): 111–17.
2. Ibid.
3. Ibid.
4. E. B. Williams, "The Great Lakes in Ancient Times and a Glimpse into the Future—Summer 1962," National Museum of the Great Lakes, June 13, 1962.
5. C. F. Michael Lewis C.F., Karrow, P.F., Blasco, S.M., McCarthy, F.M., King, J.W., Moore Jr, T.C. and Rea, D.K., "Evolution of Lakes in the Huron Basin: Deglaciation to Present," *Aquatic Ecosystem Health & Management* 11, no. 2 (2008): 127–36.
6. Ibid.
7. Michigan Sea Grant, "Supporting Habitat and Resilience in Saginaw Bay (Saginaw Bay Reef)."
8. Ashley J. Peters, "Freshwater Filter-Feeding Saginaw Bay Sees Recovery in Michigan," U.S. Fish and Wildlife Service, February 23, 2024.
9. "Bicentennial of Fort Saginaw: Consequences," Castle Museum of Saginaw County History, July 22, 2022.

10. "White Pine Logging: A Background," Geography of Michigan and the Great Lakes Region, Michigan State University.
11. "Saginaw Valley Lumbering Era," Historical Marker Database.
12. "White Pine Logging."
13. "Saginaw Valley Lumbering Era."
14. "White Pine Logging."
15. Augustus Gansser, "Greater Bay City, 1865–1905," in *History of Bay County, Michigan, and Representative Citizens*, Genealogy Trails History Group.
16. Michael Hardy, "Michigan Salt: In the 1800s, Michigan Salt from the Upper Thumb Led the Nation in Production," *Thumbwind*, December 22, 2018.
17. "Salt Brines," Geography of Michigan and the Great Lakes Region, Michigan State University.
18. Ibid.
19. U.S. Army Corps of Engineers, Great Lakes and Ohio River Division, "Saginaw River, Michigan."
20. Ibid.
21. National Transportation Safety Board (NTSB), "Marine Accident Report: Explosion and Fire Aboard the U.S. Tankship Jupiter," NTSB/MAR-91/04, 1991, 1.
22. Ibid., 18.
23. Ibid., 19.
24. Ibid., 21.
25. Ibid., 22.
26. Ibid., 26.
27. Ibid., 28.
28. Ibid.
29. Ibid.
30. "History of Bay County," Bay County, Michigan, https://www.baycountymi.gov/AboutBayCounty/HistoryBayCounty/.
31. Tim Younkman, "Bay City at 150: Lumber Ruled a Boomtown," *MLive News*, July 27, 2015.
32. Ibid.
33. Joey Oliver, "From Titanic Wreck to Presidential Yacht: Bay City Shipbuilder Left Mark on History," *MLive News*, August 31, 2024
34. "Added Prosperity Promised Bay City," Bay City, Michigan: The Way It Was, https://bcmitwiw2.wordpress.com/tag/industrial-works/.
35. Jodi Mcfarland, "Saginaw Metal Castings Operations Expansion," *MLive News*,

June 5, 2009.

36. "Added Prosperity Promised Bay City."
37. Sheryl Coonan, "Bay City's Deadly Wenonah Hotel Fire Remembered Decades Later," *ABC12 News*, December 12, 2023.
38. Andrew Dodson, "30th Anniversary of 1986 Great Flood Sparks Memories, Special Project," *MLive News*, September 12, 2016.
39. NTSB, "Explosion and Fire," 35.

Chapter 2. When Hell Visited the Saginaw River

1. NTSB, "Explosion and Fire," 5.
2. Ibid., 17.
3. Ibid.
4. Ibid., 5.
5. Ibid.
6. Ibid.
7. Ibid., 17.
8. Ibid., 5.
9. Ibid.
10. *Bay City Times* staff "Doctor Tells of Sailing Behind Buffalo," *Bay City Times*, September 30, 1990.
11. Ibid., 1.
12. Jack R. Westbrook, "History of Michigan's Oil and Natural Gas Industry," Clarke Historical Library, Central Michigan University.
13. Ibid.
14. Heidi Fearing, "John D. Rockefeller," Cleveland Historical, August 25, 2011.
15. Michael D. Roberts, "Rockefeller and His Oil Empire," Teaching Cleveland Digital, from *Inside Business*, July/August 2012.
16. Fearing, "John D. Rockefeller."
17. Roberts, "Rockefeller and His Oil Empire."
18. Chad Selweski, "Chemical Valley and the Threat to Michigan's Drinking Water," *Bridge Michigan*, October 31, 2017.
19. Kari Lydersen, "Toxic Contamination Past and Present: Creating a Legacy," Alliance for the Great Lakes, October 4, 2020.
20. Selweski, "Chemical Valley."
21. Fearing, "John D. Rockefeller."
22. Westbrook, "Michigan's Oil and Natural Gas."

23. NTSB, "Explosion and Fire," 1.
24. Ibid., 24.
25. Ibid.
26. Ibid.
27. Ibid., 28.
28. Ibid., 65.
29. Ibid., 7.
30. Ibid.
31. Ibid.
32. Ibid.
33. Ibid., 66.
34. Ibid., 10.
35. Ibid.
36. Ibid.
37. Ibid., 65.
38. Ibid., 10.
39. Ted Kleine, "The Big Question: What Caused the Ship to Explode?" *Bay City Times*, September 22, 1990.
40. "Doctor Tells of Sailing," *Bay City Times.*
41. Ted Kleine, "Ship Was Observed Throwing No Wake," *Bay City Times*, September 21, 1990.
42. Elizabeth McKenna, "Blast 'Sounded Like a Sonic Boom,'" *Bay City Times*, September 18, 1990.
43. NTSB, "Explosion and Fire," 13.
44. Jenni Laidman, "Buffalo Passes Tanker, Jupiter Later Explodes," *Bay City Times*, September 17, 1990.
45. NTSB, "Explosion and Fire," 13.
46. Ted Kleine, "Frantic Minutes Before Jupiter Blast Described," *Bay City Times*, September 26, 1990.

Chapter 3. The Wrong Place at the Right Time

1. Todd Shorkey, interview by author, July 18, 2024, Bay City, Michigan.
2. Great Lakes Vessel History, "Hackett, R. J."
3. "Grain Elevator Explosion Kills 8," *New York Times*, August 10, 1919.
4. "Fire on the Grandcamp," 1947 Texas City Disaster, Moore Memorial Public Library.

5. "Texas City, Texas, Disaster: April 16, 17, 1947," report by Fire Prevention and Engineering Bureau of Texas and National Board of Fire Underwriters.
6. NTSB, "Explosion and Fire," 41.
7. Kathy Petersen, "Heroes in Boats Rescued Seamen," *Bay City Times*, September 29, 1990.
8. Kathy Petersen, "Awards Flow Here in Wake of Jupiter Fire," *Bay City Times*, October 31, 1991.
9. NTSB, "Explosion and Fire," 38.
10. Ibid.
11. Ibid., 39.
12. Ibid., 40.
13. Ibid.
14. Shorkey interview.
15. NTSB, "Explosion and Fire," 40.
16. Kathy Petersen, "Actions of Unsung Heroes Prevented Certain Disaster," *Bay City Times*, September 15, 1991.
17. Paul Cormier, interview by author, July 18, 2024, Bay City, Michigan.

Chapter 4. Shadow Beneath the Surface

1. NTSB, "Explosion and Fire," 40.
2. Ibid.
3. Ibid.
4. U.S. Environmental Protection Agency (EPA), "Saginaw River and Bay AOC."
5. Ibid.
6. Lester Graham, "Multi-Million Dollar Restoration Projects Proposed for the Saginaw Bay Watershed; Paid with Settlement Money From Corporate Polluters," Great Lakes Now, March 22, 2023.
7. Michael Hardy, "Saginaw Bay Pollution—Alarmingly Contaminated for over 37 Years," *Thumbwind*, June 25, 2024.
8. Codi Yeager-Kozacek, "Great Lakes Water Quality: Technology and Regulations Work to Eliminate Major Shipping Pathway for Invasive Species," *Circle of Blue*, June 7, 2013.
9. Elizabeth McKenna, "Fluffy Foam Great for Snuffing Fires," *Bay City Times*, September 19, 1990.
10. Michigan Department of Environment, Great Lakes, and Energy, "PFAS," Emerging Contaminants Unit, Drinking Water and Environmental Health

Division.

11. Zoë Schlanger, "3M Has Long Known It Was Contaminating the US Food Supply," *Quartz*.
12. Jared Hayes, "'Forever Chemicals' Contamination at Defense Department Sites Threatens Great Lakes Fish and Residents," Environmental Working Group (EWG), August 31, 2021.
13. Ibid.
14. Deena Winter, "Toxic: 3M Knew Its Chemicals Were Harmful Decades Ago, but Didn't Tell the Public, Government," *Minnesota Reformer*, December 15, 2022.
15. Ibid.
16. Keith Matheny, "Internal Documents Show 3M Hid PFAS Dangers for Decades," *Detroit Free Press*, May 9, 2019.
17. Janice Carrillo, "Residents Begin Cleaning Residue from Jupiter Fire," *Bay City Times*, September 19, 1990.
18. Ibid.
19. "Black Smoke Not a Threat to the public," *Bay City Times*, September 20, 1990.
20. Ibid.
21. Ibid.
22. "We were lucky," *Bay City Times*, September 15, 1991.
23. Ibid.
24. Kathy Petersen, "Blast Killed 40,000 Fish," *Bay City Times*, August 9, 1991.
25. Ibid.
26. Elizabeth McKenna, "Gasoline Spill Cleaned Up," *Bay City Times*, September 20, 1990.
27. Kathy Petersen, "Black Liquid Leaking," *Bay City Times*, September 21, 1990.
28. Elizabeth McKenna, "Crews Scramble to Contain Black Substance," *Bay City Times*, September 22, 1990.
29. Kathy Petersen, "Removal of Gasoline from Jupiter May Start Today," *Bay City Times,* October 1, 1990.
30. Ibid.
31. Mike Turner, "Business Hurt by Shut River," *Bay City Times*, September 18, 1990.
32. Mike Turner, "Suppliers Scramble to Work Around Wreckage," *Bay City Times*, September 24, 1990.
33. Ibid.
34. Kathy Petersen, "River Is Clear," *Bay City Times*, October 22, 1990.

35. Kathy Petersen, "Jupiter Now Just About Out of Gas," *Bay City Times*, October 4, 1990.
36. "Jupiter Salvaging Continues," *Bay City Times*, October 8, 1990.
37. Kathy Petersen, "Jupiter Gets Sandbagged," *Bay City Times*, October 12, 1990.
38. Kathy Petersen, "Unusually Strong River Currents Stall Jupiter Work," *Bay City Times*, October 15, 1990.
39. Kathy Petersen, "Jupiter Is Out of Channel," *Bay City Times*, October 17, 1990.
40. Kathy Petersen, "MV Jupiter Lights Up Briefly with Fire Tuesday Night," *Bay City Times*, July 10, 1991.
41. Kathy Petersen, "Jupiter Fire Burned Up About $6.1 million," *Bay City Times*, September 15, 1991.
42. Ibid.
43. Beth McKenna and Kathy Petersen, "Jupiter Costs Soar," *Bay City Times*, September 25, 1990.
44. Peterson, "Jupiter Fire Burned Up,"
45. Ibid.
46. Michael Nowlin, "Ship Owners Deny Blame," *Bay City Times*, September 18, 1990.
47. Ibid.
48. Ibid.
49. Ibid.
50. Ted Kleine, "Buffalo's Action Called a 'Hit and Run,'" *Bay City Times*, September 19, 1990.
51. Ibid.
52. Ibid.
53. Ibid.
54. Ted Kleine, "Questions Posed in Jupiter Probe," *Bay City Times*, September 20, 1990.
55. Ibid.
56. Ibid.
57. Ibid.
58. *Bay City Times* staff, "Total, Jupiter Under Fire at Hearing," *Bay City Times*, September 30, 1990.
59. Kleine, "Throwing No wake."
60. Kleine, "What Caused Ship to Explode?" *Bay*
61. Ibid.

62. Ted Kleine, "'Buffalo Going Too Fast,'" *Bay City Times*, September 25, 1990.
63. Ibid.
64. Ibid.
65. Ted Kleine, "Jupiter Conclusions May Take Years," *Bay City Times*, September 28, 1990.
66. Ibid.
67. Ibid.
68. Kathy Petersen, "Word Still Out on Fire Causes," *Bay City Times*, September 15, 1991.
69. Mike Manger, "Dock Caused Jupiter Disaster," *Bay City Times*, October 30, 1991.

Chapter 5. The Investigation

1. NTSB, "Explosion and Fire," 44.
2. Ibid.
3. Ibid.
4. Ibid.
5. Ibid., 47.
6. Ibid., 48.
7. Ibid.
8. Ibid.
9. Ibid., 49.
10. Ibid.
11. Ibid., 50.
12. Ibid.
13. Ibid., 51.
14. Ibid.
15. Ibid.
16. Ibid.
17. Ibid.
18. Ibid., 52.
19. Ibid., 53.
20. Ibid.
21. Ibid.
22. Ibid.
23. Ibid., 54.
24. Ibid.

25. Ibid.
26. Ibid., 55.
27. Ibid.
28. Ibid.
29. Ibid., 56.
30. Ibid.
31. Ibid., 57.
32. Ibid., 58.
33. Ibid., 59.
34. Ibid.
35. Ibid., 60.

Chapter 6. Lessons Learned

1. NTSB, "Safety Recommendation to the State of Michigan," M-91-044, December 3, 1991.
2. Official correspondence from State of Michigan to NTSB, April 21, 1998.
3. NTSB, "Safety Recommendation to County of Bay, Emergency Services," M-91-045, December 3, 1991.
4. Official correspondence from NTSB to State of Michigan, County of Bay, Emergency Services, February 10, 1994.
5. NTSB, "Safety Recommendation to County of Bay."
6. NTSB, "Safety Recommendation to Lake Carriers' Association," M-91-043, December 3, 1991.
7. Ibid.
8. Ibid.
9. Ibid.
10. Official correspondence from Lake Carriers' Association to NTSB, June 24, 1992.
11. Official correspondence from NTSB to Lake Carriers' Association, August 31, 1992.
12. Lake Carriers' Association to NTSB, September 22, 1992.
13. NTSB to Lake Carriers' Association, November 12, 1992.
14. NTSB, "Safety Recommendation to Total Petroleum, Inc.," M-91-030-042, December 3, 1991.
15. Official correspondence from NTSB to Total Petroleum Inc., April 10, 1992.
16. NTSB to Total Petroleum, February 18, 1993.
17. NTSB, "Safety Recommendation to Cleveland Tankers, Inc.," M-91-038,

December 3, 1991.

18. NTSB, "Safety Recommendation to Cleveland Tankers, Inc.," M-91-037, December 3, 1991.
19. NTSB, "Recommendation to Cleveland Tankers," M-91-038.
20. Official correspondence from Cleveland Tankers to NTSB, March 29, 1993..
21. NTSB, "Safety Recommendation to USCG [U.S. Coast Guard]," M-91-036, December 3, 1991.
22. Ibid.
23. Official correspondence from USCG to NTSB, July 10, 1992.
24. Official correspondence from NTSB to USCG, March 20, 1997.
25. Official correspondence from NTSB to USCG, October 6, 1992.
26. Official correspondence from NTSB to USCG, March 20, 1997.
27. Official correspondence from NTSB to USCG, October 29, 2001.

Index